15 Years of Panic Attacks
Sara Müller

Bibliographic Information of the German National Library: The German National Library lists this publication in the German National Bibliography; detailed bibliographic data can be accessed online via dnb. dnb.de.

Original title: 15 Jahre Panikattacken. Die Haupttrigger waren Histamin und Gluten!

Translation and Editing: Stefanie Simmler, Switzerland
Layout and Typesetting: Herrn Meyers Buchmacherei, Germany
Photographer: Simoni Tardin, Italy
Publisher: BoD · Books on Demand GmbH, In de Tarpen 42, 22848 Norderstedt
Print: Libri Plureos GmbH, Friedensallee 273, 22763 Hamburg
ISBN: 978-3-7693-0869-3

SARA MÜLLER

15 YEARS
OF PANIC ATTACKS

The Main Triggers Were Histamine and Gluten!

BIOGRAPHY, GUIDE AND COOKBOOK

FOREWORD

Dear Reader,

I warmly welcome you and would like to share with you in this book how I suffered from panic attacks for years without even knowing that this feeling of anxiety had a name. Rarely do people talk about it; instead, they hide and live with makeshift solutions.

My journey of suffering and finding a solution took fifteen years. I want to spare you such a long path and, based on my own biography, illustrate: What are the warning signs? What "traps" arise from one-sided diagnoses? How do panic attacks manifest as the "final stage" of undiagnosed histamine intolerance and gluten sensitivity? Ultimately, I want to clarify that purely psychological treatment of panic attacks did not lead to their disappearance for me.

The good thing about panic attacks is that they act as a guide, like a final "warning" before you hit a dead end. They are by no means "evil," but rather a sign from your body that you need to change your life because warning signs were apparently not seen, overlooked, or even consciously ignored. The body then pulls the emergency brake with panic attacks. Your psyche or soul is showing you that something is wrong. Neither your brain nor anything else in you is damaged; panic attacks are simply a warning system of your body.

Fate has led you to this book, and perhaps here you will find answers or even opportunities to steer your life in a new direction.

I sought help and received it, and I would now like to pass this on to you.

Sara Mueller
www.higlutrigger.ch

TABLE OF CONTENTS

55 INFORMATION AND KNOWLEDGE

Table of contents

91 TIPS, RECIPES, FOOD LIST, WEEKLY PLAN

CHILDHOOD AND TEENAGER YEARS

Sometime in late 2019, my husband and I were invited to a birthday party. On the invitation, you could choose whether you wanted a vegetarian, vegan, or lactose-free menu. Back then, it seemed like a huge trend to me; all these options made me smile.

Had I only taken better care of my diet beforehand, I could have avoided some panic attacks, I know that much now.

But one thing at a time, because after all, I come from Bern, and we Bernese are known for our rather slow pace.

I grew up with my parents, my younger sister, and seven Greek tortoises living in the garden, for whom I had great respect. Every time I got near them, I felt something, but I couldn't identify it and thus called it "fear." From a young age, I was simply afraid of tortoises and kept my distance whenever possible. I was also very sensitive, and my surroundings referred to me as such. In contrast to the rest of my family, I was rather shy and reserved. I always wished I could be much braver one day, to show the world that I wasn't such a "softie."

But my health didn't cooperate. At the age of five, I had my first pneumonia, followed by three more by the end of my school years. As a infant I also had many allergies, which varied in severity. Various allergy tests, yielded no results.

Throughout my school years, I endured many asthma attacks, the cause of which the doctors could never identify despite frequent examinations. It was neither allergic nor exercise-induced asthma. As was common at the time, I received an asthma inhaler to alleviate the attacks. For many weeks, I couldn't even make it home without needing to use my inhaler immediately upon arrival.

School, the Teachers, My Parents…the Entire Pressure to Perform Was Too Much for Me.

I found a wonderful balance in painting and making music, especially on the keyboard. Somehow, I played songs by ear, without being able to read music. I explained to those around me that I saw my surroundings and the music in special shapes and colors. No one believed me.

Fortunately, volleyball training helped me keep my body fit. I even played in the U-20 team and trained up to four times a week. Matches often took place on weekends. During puberty, new strengths suddenly emerged, making me feel strong and brave. The long-standing cliché of being too sensitive began to change slowly as my drive for achievement kicked in. At the same time, I started modeling.

1. Alcohol Taboo and Medications with Caution

During my apprenticeship as a construction drafter, I fell in love with a singer who was very well-known in his home country of Italy. After receiving my professional diploma, I decided to move directly to Milan (Italy), much to the dismay of my parents. With two suitcases and a lot of courage, I set off.

The following two years were some of the best times of my life. It was fascinating to discover the warm Italian culture and this lifestyle that was so different from that of Switzerland. With my boyfriend, I traveled all over Italy as he had concerts every two days. During tour breaks, I interned at architecture firms in Milan or worked as a model for fashion shows and photo shoots. I got insights into the world of paparazzi, bodyguards, and castings, of assignments and parties. I also quickly learned the Italian language, which was previously unknown to me.

When I started consuming alcohol, I quickly noticed that my body did not react well to it. It was a strange feeling that came over me: dizziness, heart palpitations, and I had to hold on to keep my balance. Even a small "Kirschstängeli" triggered these symptoms. In short, it was almost unbearable to take alcohol. The same applied to medications - almost every medication seemed too strong for me. Even for headaches, I only took half a tablet to avoid being overwhelmed by side effects. It was a challenge to find the right balance between effective treatment and unpleasant side effects, and I always had to be careful not to trigger unwanted reactions.

I hardly paid attention to these symptoms since they were not "life-limiting". When people offered me a glass of wine, I always replied that I did not drink alcohol. Sometimes the reaction was: "Wow, how can you have fun and be cheerful then?" There was only one reply: "I enjoy the evening even without alcohol." Honestly, to this day, I don't understand why one needs wine to be cheerful.

Looking back, the intolerance of alcohol and the limited tolerance of medications were the first signs that histamine breakdown was not functioning as it should.

My love for painting remained. In my free time, I painted as often as I could. In Florence, one of my paintings was even exhibited. Health-wise, I felt sensational. All allergies and asthma seem to have magically disappeared. Only stomach aches plagued me now and then. Looking back, it was probably due to the abundant pasta and a case of gluten sensitivity.

At some point, I realized that this lifestyle did not fulfill me. It would certainly have been a dream life for many. But my inner voice told me that I had to take new paths. So, I decided to study architecture. Returning to Switzerland, I began my studies at the Technical University in Winterthur. The quick switch from Milan's jet-set lifestyle to student life was very challenging, but I managed it a period of time. In comparison to Switzerland, I missed the warm-hearted culture of the South. Therefore, I traveled all over Europe and America whenever time allowed. In Paris (France), I met a band with whom I even tried my luck as a singer. This created a balance between heart and mind for me.

During my architecture studies, digitalization made its entry. Our drawing table, where the most beautiful, creative, ink-drawn plans had been made, was replaced by a laptop with drawing programs. Since I was not a big IT fan, the creative part of architecture studies came to an end for me.

Although I worked for some time in an architecture firm after graduation, I soon realized that it was simply not suitable for me to plan "only" on a computer with 3D programs instead of drawing by hand. Personal communication with clients and specialists was often reduced to just emails. The profession of an architect had changed significantly since the beginning of my studies. Once more, I had to find a solution.

2. Unexplained Abdominal Cramps

Through a career start program at a major bank, I was able to have more personal contact with people again. There, I tried to better understand the economy, society, and their power imbalances. Through the program, I worked in various departments, including real estate, sales, consulting, and appraisal of properties. Then I switched to the "internal police," the so-called Business Risk Management. My backpack of experiences quickly filled up, and I always encountered new challenges.

At the same time, my allergies resurfaced, first mainly through intestinal problems. I even had to go to the emergency room twice due to piercing, unbearable stomach cramps. A CT scan, ultrasound examinations, and various blood tests were done. But no cause could be found, and I was sent home again.

From today's perspective, with the current knowledge, I probably lost the balance between heart and mind back then. Due to a lack of time, I focused mainly on my mind during my work in Switzerland. The mental imbalance and improper diet gradually damaged my intestines. This seems to have been the cause of the stomach cramps.

3. The First Time

From time to time, I could indulge my creative side a bit through exhibitions of my painted works at home and abroad. I exhibited at Art International in Zurich, Art Berlin, or Artexpo in New York.

And there, in New York, something terrible happened to me. My parents, who had also come along, went on a sightseeing tour while I sat on a chair next to my works. Hundreds of people buzzed past me. Suddenly, my heart raced. I got dizzy and was terribly scared, real deathly fear, out of nowhere. Then I fainted.

Paramedics took me to a side room. My parents immediately returned to me. My attack was inexplicable. It was assumed that I was probably a bit dehydrated. The days that followed were an absolute horror. I was scared when I had to go back to the many people in the exhibition box, and the feeling got stronger and stronger. My family took over the exhibition duties for me while I lay in the hotel bed. No one knew exactly what I had, including myself. The terrible feeling of anxiety just appeared and made my heart race.

Looking back, this was my first, unrecognized panic attack. Back in Switzerland, I underwent a comprehensive health check, including an ECG and allergy test. All tests confirmed that my body was in excellent condition. So, I continued my work, additionally taking on the leadership of a team and was appointed as a lecturer at the Business School.

Today I know that panic attacks should be considered as warning signs from the body. They showed me that I should have changed my path immediately. The attacks were, so to speak, the emergency brake of my body. I ignored all these signs by just continuing to work and live as usual.

1. The Situation Is Deteriorating

When I met my husband, I was a real businesswoman: I worked successfully at a major bank as a Senior Risk Manager. In my free time, I painted and exhibited my works at home and abroad. Since the experience in New York, this strange feeling always accompanied me. At that time, I lived in a small apartment in Zurich. This frightening feeling overtook me again in the evenings when I was quietly at home. An inexplicable pulsing coupled with heart palpitations ran through my body. Then came great fear, the heart palpitations got worse until I fainted. Experiencing this alone at home plunged me into even greater panic.

From that moment on, I tried not to come home earlier than my husband, to avoid being alone at home in the evening. As a "strong" businesswoman, I could not tell anyone about this, and no one would have believed me anyway. Moreover, I was embarrassed by my condition.

Since I knew nothing about panic attacks at the time, the phenomenon of fear of fear was also unknown to me.

2. Fainting from a Cocktail

In 2009, my now-husband and I booked a beautiful spring vacation in the Maldives. He was a trained dive guide and wanted to show me the wonderful underwater world of the islands. I had not had any underwater adventures until then; I had always sailed or surfed on the water. Indeed, a dream island awaited me with a beautiful sandy beach and turquoise sea.

After the first two days, I already suffered from a painful sun allergy, despite factor-50 sunscreen and lots of shade. From then on, I went to the beach in a long-sleeved shirt and long pants from then on. The unfortunate first attempts with the oxygen tank to dive brought back bad memories of the inhalation device from my asthma days. Gradually, I overcame my difficulties and enjoyed the underwater world.

One day we planned a diving excursion to see sharks. As soon as the boat arrived at a suitable spot, all the divers slipped into their suits. At that moment, two fears arose in me: On the one hand, I had great respect for the sharks (which was somehow justified...), on the other hand, if I stayed here alone with the boat captain in the open sea, then. .. and the feeling of fear was back.

I decided to follow the group and swim to the sharks because the fear of staying alone on the boat outweighed the respect for the sharks. During this excursion, eight sharks swam around and over us. To endure this, I clung tightly to my husband's hand.

In the evening at the bar, many people reminisced about this sensational shark dive. Although I had told my husband several times before that I could not tolerate alcohol, he ordered me a long drink with rum. He simply did not believe that someone could not tolerate alcohol at all. So, I drank about half of it. When I stood up to go to dinner, I got dizzy and...

When I regained consciousness, three men were leaning over me, and someone was pressing an oxygen mask to my mouth. My husband was holding my hand and asked worriedly if I could see and hear him. After a while, I recovered, and they explained to me that I had fainted right by the bar. I wanted to know from my beloved if he now believed that I couldn't handle alcohol. Pushing my wheelchair through the sand, he brought me to our bungalow. The remaining days passed without any major incidents.

3. The Thing Has a Name

After returning from vacation, I finally decided to see a psychologist, even though my pride was initially against it. For the first time, I heard the term "panic attack" and learned that these frightening feelings were called that! They manifested as sudden fear, accompanied by rapid heartbeat, chest tightness, dizziness, and even fainting. This matched my experiences exactly, the psychologist explained to me.

After this diagnosis, I had to accept that I had a "psychological problem." I decided to share this with only a few selected people. I knew I had to reduce stress. This meant cutting back on my hobby, as I believed there was no room for compromise in my professional life. So, I painted less and stopped participating in exhibitions. Only today do I realize how much this decision threw me off balance.

4. A Vicious Circle

The wedding was approaching. On May 8, 2010, we celebrated a dream wedding at the Münster Bern. During the preparation phase, I was increasingly overcome by feelings of anxiety. In the supermarket, while waiting at the checkout, my heart would suddenly start racing. In the elevator, I felt trapped and confined, so I preferred to take the stairs. At home alone, I fainted again. This further intensified the panic until I began to avoid such situations. I either arranged for the neighbor to keep me company or tried to come home later than my husband.

Like the people around me, I assumed that the nervousness before the wedding was the cause. I tried to avoid these experiences with new tactics. All this gnawed at my self-esteem. On the one hand, I could easily give an interesting lecture to 300 people as a speaker, but on the other hand, I was unable to spend an hour alone at home.

Later, in therapy, I learned that avoiding such situations would only increase the fear and lead to the so-called fear of fear - a vicious circle.

Six months after our wedding, our dream honeymoon was supposed to begin: After an exciting safari tour, a relaxing vacation by the sea in Zanzibar was to follow. But fate had other plans. Three days before the honeymoon, I was driving my car through the streets of Zurich. Suddenly, I felt a strong heartbeat. My arms grew heavy. Everything started to spin. Instinctively and quickly, I steered the car onto the sidewalk, brought it to a stop, opened the door, and called my husband. But the words got stuck in my throat. I lost consciousness.

What happened next, I only learned from stories. Apparently, the ambulance took me to the emergency room, accompanied by my husband. When I came to in a bed in the emergency room, the doctors revealed the bitter diagnosis based on the examinations: burnout with anxiety disorder.

I felt deep relief that I had survived this terrible incident. No one was harmed due to my timely evasive action. The diagnosis of burnout weighed heavily on me. And, of course, it was sad to have to cancel the honeymoon.

The weeks that followed required nerves of steel, and I spent a lot of time at home. Unfortunately, in the following 13 years, we were unable to reschedule our honeymoon. Nevertheless, I am confident that we will one day enjoy it together.

5. The Way Back

A stay in a clinic was out of the question for me, as I did not see myself as mentally ill. As a successful businesswoman, it seemed unthinkable to retreat behind the walls of a clinic. Instead, I spent the following months at home. A demanding job at the large bank was far off, while I focused on finding a new rhythm in life. My path also led me to a psychiatrist. There, I was prescribed psychotropic drugs to treat the panic attacks and we explored the roots of my fears through conversations.

Due to the incident in the car, I had developed the classic "fear of fear." Step by step, I tried to regain trust. Slowly, I started using elevators and trams again, waited in line at the store checkout, and walked alone outside without patient accompaniment. All this increasingly succeeded without panic attacks. This became a major challenge to overcome once again. Persistently, I relearned to perform everyday tasks, this time freed from the burden of fears.

The process required a considerable amount of strength and courage. After six months, I finally returned to my job at the bank. Unfortunately, I continued at the same pace as before.

1. Baby Joys with Problems

A year later, I became pregnant. My husband and I were overjoyed. In the sixth month, the gynecologist diagnosed that the baby had dropped. To prevent premature birth, I was immediately taken from the doctor's office to the hospital. There, I was prescribed absolute bed rest. So, I lay there, confined to bed, day after day with no chance of escape. Panic attacks struck me again.

Fortunately, the joy of the baby prevailed. In 2012, our daughter was born healthy and lively. During the maternity leave, a lot happened. The feelings were like a roller coaster ride during the days at home. Parenthood turned our lives upside down, not only because of the need to think about diapers or getting up in the middle of the night to feed the hungry baby. The birth of my daughter also triggered emotions within me that I had not known before. Motherhood awakened a sensitivity in me that was previously unfamiliar. This emotional turmoil triggered new panic attacks.

At the same time, due to various circumstances, my husband had to look for a new professional challenge. It was really an inconvenient time to change jobs, with a little princess at home, the new life as a family, and a wife with strained nerves.

Thanks to the help and support of our families, we managed this challenge very well. My husband found an exciting job, and I re-entered the large bank through job sharing. This work model involved sharing a job with leadership responsibilities among two or more people. For me, it meant living part of the day as a businesswoman and the other part as a mom.

Why I was warmly welcomed as a businesswoman in the city of Zurich at a café in the morning and not in the afternoon as a mom with a stroller was beyond me. As a person with many ideas, I tried to get to the bottom of the problem and find solutions. I founded my first company. For this, I wrote a guide about baby- and child-friendly cafés in Zurich, designed a Mammaconnect pin, and distributed play boxes to entertain children in cafés, financed through crowdfunding. I wanted to combat the loneliness of mothers.

In a newspaper interview, the journalist wanted to know how I came up with the idea. I explained: "I see a problem, then a kind of puzzle with colors, words, and shapes appears in my mind. Intuitively, the right solution forms in my head. I see the world in lines, shapes, colors, and patterns." Laughing, I continued: "You won't believe it, but I also see words in color." "Oh, so you're a synesthete!" came the reply.

Wow, there was actually a word for it? Until then, I had either been labeled as odd or simply not believed when I talked about my perception.

I immediately began to explore the topic of synesthesia. Finally, I could describe myself as "normal." It was a gift, a special expression of natural forms of perception. For once, I found myself in a socially recognized category and could explain it to my family and friends so they better understood who I was.

The balancing act between work and private life became increasingly larger. Many mothers are exposed to this enormous stress. Panic attacks increased, and the psychiatrist at the time could not do much. So, I decided to leave the bank after 11 years and become self-employed. This way, I hoped to at least be able to make my working hours more flexible.

But precisely the lack of opportunities to combine work and family was the reason to found the company Jobsharing-Consulting MS AG.

The goal was to make job sharing more known in Switzerland and encourage companies to adopt the model. After my maternity leave, I had experienced it myself and found it very good to be able to keep my job but work with a reduced workload.

Many people showed great interest. They wanted to live exactly this work model. I started the first Jobsharing-Speed-Network in Zurich. I also founded a platform for job-sharing partners to meet and build partnerships with renowned organizations. My guide on the subject was very well received. At the same time, I was able to share my knowledge on "Better Work-Life Balance" as a speaker and panelist at various institutions.

2. Moving Forward

Despite this success, my allergies worsened: After eating hummus, my face turned red and swollen. After eating an avocado, I found myself on the ground. Today I know that chickpeas and avocados contain a lot of histamine. Due to severe lower abdominal pain, I had to go to the hospital twice. The CT scan and all other examinations showed nothing unusual; since my abdominal muscles were tense, I was recommended physiotherapy.

Once, due to the severe pain, I was prescribed Novalgin, a pain-relieving medication. Shortly after picking up the medication from the pharmacy, I took it. Soon after, I became dizzy and lost consciousness on the sidewalk. A passerby called the ambulance, which took me to the hospital.

The doctors found that I had an overreaction to Novalgin. After a short recovery, they discharged me home. Now, my psychiatrist recommended an allergy test. The result: Atopic, which means someone who reacts strongly with allergic reactions to normally harmless substances or environmental stimuli.

With My Life, I Continued as Usual. The illusion of flexible time management in self-employment soon ended. Working hours increased, and the desired free time dwindled. Parallel to this, panic attacks became more frequent. Xanthelasmas, yellow deposits that typically indicate high cholesterol, suddenly appeared under my eyes and on my upper eyelid. Since I never drank alcohol and wasn't overweight, a blood lipid test was conducted. The results were normal, so there was no explanation for the development of xanthelasmas.

FROM THE CITY TO THE COUNTRYSIDE

1. Adjustment of Living Conditions

Because mold was spreading in our city apartment and our daughter began to suffer from asthma, we decided to move to the fresh country air. After more than twenty years in big cities like Milan, Paris, or Zurich, I took the plunge into the Zurich Oberland. My friends gave me only a few months, as they knew me as a "round-the-clock" action woman, enjoying city life and the many people.

To my surprise, we settled in quickly. Our daughter liked the countryside much better than the noisy city. My husband, who had only moved to the city for me, was also happy. I, on the other hand, had to find my footing first. Through new contacts and acquaintances, especially with other families, my perspective changed. And I began to enjoy the benefits of rural life with a child.

The change of seasons was particularly impressive. While in the city you mostly saw interiors, now I could observe the weather, nature, and the changing seasons through the window. I noticed when the birds migrated south and when they returned. My work took a backseat, and people, family, became the focus. I discovered my green thumb by starting a vegetable garden. Everything grew wonderfully, and I enjoyed our own tomatoes, radishes, cucumbers, and zucchinis.

In the community, I wanted to contribute constructively and got elected to the municipal council. My day was filled with work for two companies, the council, the garden, and, of course, the most important role, being a mom. Occasionally, my back let me know it was losing strength, but I didn't listen, which I paid for with a lumbago.

Unfortunately, my panic attacks didn't disappear, which truly surprised me. I had tried all possible ways: with various psychologists, with or without medication, even with a change of residence.

2. The Enlightenment

By chance or rather fate, I was recommended a new doctor. After we got to know each other better, I felt cared for by a psychiatrist for the first time. Within a short time, he not only examined my blood but also analyzed my stool and urine. He inquired extensively about my medical history and illuminated aspects that had previously been overlooked. Keeping a food diary over a certain period proved to be very effective. I noted what I had eaten and whether any symptoms followed.

Together, we analyzed the entries. It was November 2019, and his diagnosis was astonishing: **histamine intolerance and gluten sensitivity**.

Histamine intolerance describes exceeding the personal tolerance limit for histamine, leading to an excessive burden on the organism. Symptoms can include headaches, skin rashes, digestive problems, panic attacks, depression, and more, as detailed from page 77. My doctor explained that he had encountered many patients who reacted to food intolerance with depression or anxiety disorders.

In gluten sensitivity, there is a hypersensitivity to gluten or other grain components, without corresponding changes in the intestinal mucosa or allergic changes in the immune system. Symptoms of gluten sensitivity can include abdominal pain, diarrhea, skin rashes, depression, panic attacks, and more, as detailed from page 85.

That was my great AHA MOMENT! These insights allowed me to look back on my life from a new perspective: Hadn't I reacted with allergies since childhood? Didn't I suffer from inexplicable asthma? Didn't abdominal pains follow, for which there was no diagnosis? Couldn't I tolerate alcohol either? Didn't strange feelings of anxiety and panic attacks follow consumption?

Suddenly, everything made sense. Above all, it relieved me that I wasn't just prone to panic attacks for psychological reasons but probably due to a physical defect. For this incredible aha experience, I am still grateful to my doctor.

3. One Is Noticed, the Other Less

Histamine intolerance and gluten sensitivity can only be confirmed by eliminating certain foods. I delved deeply into both topics and gradually changed my diet.

> **You are what you eat.**
> Brillat-Savarin, *The Physiology of Taste*, 1826

But after frequently reading that Daosin tablets could regulate histamine levels, I didn't pay much more attention to this topic and regularly took the tablets.

Regarding gluten, I behaved differently. I informed myself about which foods contained gluten and tried to replace them with gluten-free alternatives. Replacing foods, required a significant amount of time.

For example: Baking gluten-free bread was real research work, as I had to combine different flours like teff flour, rice flour, and almond flour, add the right starch - cornstarch or tapioca starch - and, depending on the flour mix, choose a binding agent like guar gum or locust bean gum. The icing on the cake was then deciding whether to use yeast or a yeast substitute. Depending on the ingredients, the finished bread tasted quite different.

In the shopping center, I was convinced by gluten-free pasta. Although there were significant taste differences depending on the brand and ingredients, I found a gluten-free pasta that smelled good to me.

Simultaneously preparing "normal" meals for my husband and daughter and gluten-free dishes for myself took a lot of time. With the dietary change to gluten-free and the Daosin tablets for histamine intolerance, my panic attacks improved.

In subsequent doctor consultations, I gained further insights: After various rounds of questions and tests, the doctor diagnosed me with high sensitivity. As a highly sensitive person, you have the ability to perceive the environment more intensely and accurately, which can sometimes be very stressful. There it was again, the sentence from early childhood: "You are sensitive." The explanation that high sensitivity should not be seen as a disease—something negative—but as a trait, surprised me. But since I was already spending so much time on dietary changes in my everyday life, I let this topic rest for the time being.

4. A Severe Setback

The exciting Christmas season and New Year's Eve passed. I had come to terms with the new insights and had just started to study them when the battle against the coronavirus began.

We were practically locked up, and that triggered a downward spiral in me. The feeling of being trapped created a need to flee. This led to a sense of hopelessness, and my body responded with palpitations, sweating, trembling, and shortness of breath, eventually culminating in a panic attack.

The situation escalated until fear took over. In April 2020, I lost eleven kilograms in one month, and panic attacks overwhelmed me daily. At some point, my body shut down, and I just sat there motionless. Admitted to a psychiatric clinic as an emergency, my diagnosis was once again: burnout with anxiety disorder.

There I was in a clinic, something I had always wanted to avoid. These weeks would turn out to be one of the best times of my life. I felt like I was in an empty space, without time and pressure. Although I missed my husband and daughter terribly, as they were not allowed to visit me due to the corona rules at the time, I could reflect, orient myself, let my body rest, and I learned a lot about myself.

The first thing I learned was that I had forgotten how to breathe properly. Yes, you read that right. Due to the constant stress of recent years, I had adopted shallow breathing. So, I had to relearn how to breathe deeply into my belly. To this day, breathing exercises are part of my daily ritual because they calm the sympathetic nervous system and activate the parasympathetic nervous system, leading the body into a state of rest and recovery: Slowly and deeply breathe into the abdomen, counting to three, slowly exhale, counting to five.

At first, mindfulness exercises didn't appeal to me at all. But soon I learned to appreciate the calm and power of the "now" and didn't constantly drift into future planning or the past with my thoughts.

I had to learn to endure panic attacks without taking emergency medication. During this time, I experienced that although the fear was huge and my body was in a state of alarm, I would not die.

The vicious cycle of thoughts needed to be broken. I started incorporating breaks into my day because I had previously removed them from my daily routine due to time pressure. Over the past few years, I had stopped painting due to a lack of time. Now I realized that this very activity became a source of balance and relaxation. Even today, I diligently practice incorporating breaks into my day and not neglecting them. This keeps the body, mind, and soul in balance.

I reacted to the medication prescribed to me in the clinic with severe panic attacks; it was a very difficult time. With the help of a genetic test, it was determined what was compatible with me. Ultimately, a suitable psychotropic drug was found, but it had to be administered in very low doses. Today I know that many medications are unsuitable for those with histamine intolerance.

During my stay in the clinic, I looked inward more frequently. I got to know myself better. Surprisingly many things I had liked until then turned out to be wrong. For example, I thought I was a city person, having always lived in cities and loved the city noise. I had only used this noise to silence the inner voice, which then led to complete sensory overload for my body.

I learned to accept my high sensitivity and not to hide it. Why should I? If one has gifts and is aware of their drawbacks, one should also appreciate the positive aspects. High sensitivity is not a disease but a trait. It is estimated that 20% of people are highly sensitive. They have fine antennas and a highly sensitive nervous system, enabling them to notice subtle nuances in their surroundings.

Highly sensitive people are very active, committed, and sociable. Due to their sensitivity, they perceive more than other people, which can lead to sensory overload. Often, they do not know that they are highly sensitive and are puzzled by their occasional physical or emotional breakdowns.

Information is processed much more thoroughly. As a result, highly sensitive people are often visionaries because they have an idea of "the bigger picture." They also tend to have more allergies and react strongly to medications (Wyrsch, 2020), (Hochsensibilität, 2023), (Schauwecker, 2023), (Zoller, 2023).

I also learned a lot about panic attacks: they serve as signposts and last warnings before one hits a dead end. They are not "evil" signals but indicate that the path needs to be changed immediately. Panic attacks function as an emergency brake, showing that changes are necessary and that previous signs may have been overlooked or deliberately ignored. It is as if the soul is showing the body that one has gone off course.

As a result, I realized that I needed to completely realign my life situation. I found this good; the stay in the clinic felt as if someone had unplugged me and then reprogrammed me.

> **Whoever has overcome their fears will truly be free.**
> Aristotle (384-322 BC)

1. The Realignment

During my time at the clinic, I indicated "histamine intolerance and gluten sensitivity" on the food list, although I was still in the "trial phase." Nevertheless, I attended the clinic's nutritional counseling. There, they confirmed the connection between diet and panic attacks. Since I was taking Daosin tablets for histamine intolerance, together with the counselor, I decided to initially eliminate gluten from my diet.

After several weeks of recuperation at the clinic, I felt it was time to completely realign my professional life situation. I reset my "work life" to zero. I immediately closed down my two companies and resigned from my position as a municipal councilor. Despite the initial unfamiliarity, this decision was liberating and opened up the opportunity for me to finally focus on myself. Without pressure to perform, without stress, and without fixed appointments, a space emerged where I could rediscover my balance.

Back at home, I faced the challenge of relearning everyday actions from scratch. Day by day, I tackled my tasks and diligently trained not to be overwhelmed by panic attacks at every step, such as when boarding the subway. I overcame the fear of being alone at home, of fainting, and I conquered many other hurdles. I bravely fought through each day, and slowly but surely, things started to improve.

In the summer, through a colleague, I met a naturopath who supported me from a complementary perspective. On one hand, he helped me rebuild my damaged gut; on the other hand, he contributed to calming my overall body and much more.

Suddenly, I was "just" a mom by profession, which occasionally felt strange but was tremendous solace for my nerves. I continued to find my balance through painting.

By chance, a gallery in New York discovered my paintings, and I was able to participate in a group exhibition. Shortly after, I even had the opportunity to exhibit in a museum in South Korea. The rest of the year 2020 was simply beautiful, stress-free, and passed without any panic attacks.

2. An Unexpected Setback

In the summer of 2021, I was again plagued by severe abdominal cramps. When they became unbearable, I went to the emergency room. Doctors conducted various tests, from EKGs to ultrasounds and a gynecological check, but they found nothing conclusive. It was truly confusing to receive no diagnosis despite intense pain.

Eventually, I consulted my naturopath who identified a significant imbalance in my gut bacteria. A healthy gut hosts a diverse community of bacteria, and disruptions can lead to various problems. My naturopath recommended natural remedies to restore my gut flora.

Shortly afterward, I woke up in the middle of the night and collapsed almost immediately upon standing. When I regained consciousness, my husband was by my side, caring for me lovingly. It troubled me deeply that I could faint without warning. What was happening to my body?

I visited the doctor and subsequently had to take and record my blood pressure every morning and evening for a week. The readings showed significant fluctuations. The doctor diagnosed physical weakness as the cause of my fainting spells.

I wondered, if the fainting spell was due to physical weakness, could it be that the panic attacks were also "just" a result of this physical weakness and not a "psychological problem"?

To gain more clarity, I underwent a 24-hour EKG and comprehensive blood tests. The EKG showed no abnormalities, but my iron levels were very low, and my blood sugar levels indicated early signs of diabetes. In response, I reduced my sugar intake and started taking supplements. This led to noticeable improvement in my abdominal cramps, and I no longer experienced fainting spells.

3. Rejoicing Too Soon

In 2022, I focused on achieving balance between my inner and outer self, between body and soul. I felt very well, so much so that I even began tapering off the medications prescribed to me at the clinic. Feeling that my mind and body were healthy, I thought I could resume eating everything. I joyfully celebrated Christmas without restrictions and enjoyed birthday cakes at numerous parties. I was thrilled with my good fortune: no more panic attacks, and I didn't need to monitor my food intake anymore. Occasionally, I experienced gastrointestinal discomfort, but I assumed it would resolve itself.

However, disillusionment struck in early March 2023. As I was about to go to bed, my body started trembling. Suddenly, after such a long time, another panic attack? The trembling persisted, my entire body shook, my thoughts raced, I felt nauseous, and I was gripped by intense fear.

Not even emergency medications helped. I was on the verge of calling an ambulance when I vomited. After vomiting again, I started to feel slightly better.

The memory of that night weighed heavily on me, triggering daily panic attacks once again. Additionally, I almost stopped sleeping and lost ten kilograms in a short period. A panic attack felt to my body like climbing a 2000-meter-high mountain.

It felt like I had been transported back to the year 2020. Did I really have to experience everything all over again? I was at the end of my strength.

4. Starting Over with Two New Terms

In conversation with my doctor, it became clear that behind my persistent symptoms lay an unresolved challenge: histamine intolerance "and" gluten sensitivity. This condition didn't simply disappear on its own, and the stomach cramps and digestive issues were quite unmistakable!

It hit me like a blow – after all, I had been living without any special restrictions for six months! Yet now my gut was reacting: the leaky gut syndrome. Leaky gut syndrome refers to an increasing permeability of the intestinal wall, allowing unwanted substances to enter the bloodstream. With histamine intolerance, the body reacts with a histamine attack; with gluten sensitivity, it's a gluten attack, more on that from page 77.

So, what I had dismissed as a panic attack on that dreadful night in March was actually either a severe histamine attack or a gluten attack. Both terms were completely new to me. The initial symptoms were remarkably similar: rapid heartbeat, abdominal pain, diarrhea, nausea, and a racing pulse – a combination that could easily mimic an impending panic attack. My mind raised the alarm, but in reality, it was an overreaction to histamine or gluten.

Simply taking Daosin tablets wasn't enough to gain control over histamine intolerance. That became painfully clear to me. The time had come to start over and consistently follow a gluten-free "and" low-histamine diet. This time, I took both intolerances seriously and delved deeper into the topic of histamine intolerance.

In my research, I learned that histamine is not only absorbed through food but can also be produced within the body by extreme temperatures, excessive exercise, or even intense odors such as those found in spice markets.

The world of intolerances unfolded before me like a fascinating yet challenging cosmos.

"All diseases begin in the gut."
Hippocrates (5th century BC)

---

5. What Low-Histamine and Gluten-Free Means

To make sure I did everything right this time, I wanted to consider "both" intolerances. That meant for me:

Low-Histamine in brief
- No fermentation and fermentation products (for example, alcohol, vinegar, yeast)
- No long-warmed or reheated foods
- Thaw quickly and use immediately! Do not thaw slowly in the refrigerator.
- Observe no preservatives, dyes, acidulants, E-list, etc.
- No canned goods, no ready-made or semi-prepared products (no yeast extract)
- Only fresh goods (especially for fish and meat), if possible, no packaged goods
- Meat not minced or chopped, only whole pieces. Depending on personal tolerance, you can chop the meat yourself before frying.
- Be careful with spices: No lemons, no pepper, mustard and soy, chili and salt only iodine-free
- Pay attention to special food lists for histamine intolerance (no spinach, tomatoes, strawberries, pineapple, etc.)

Gluten-free in brief
- Gluten is present in most types of grains: wheat, spelt, rye, barley, bulgur, couscous, and khorasan wheat (kamut).
- Therefore, normal baked goods and pasta (bread, pizza, pasta, etc.) contain gluten.
- Gluten is used as a stabilizer, thickener, gelling agent, flavor enhancer, etc.
- Gluten is also found in all malt-containing (barley) foods, such as beer, malt coffee, or similar.
- Gluten can also be hidden in toothpaste, chocolate, ready-made sauces, chips, and flavor enhancers.

6. Dietary Change - Confusion, Helplessness, Exhaustion

Despite numerous books on gluten sensitivity and others on histamine intolerance, I couldn't find one that specifically addressed the needs of individuals with both histamine intolerance and gluten sensitivity. Thus, the first few days were difficult because I no longer knew what I was allowed to eat. If a food was positively rated on one list, it was the opposite on the other. If an ingredient was recommended on one list, the opposite was true on the other.

I survived on rice, potatoes, apples, and oatmeal. I lost another six kilograms. I grew weaker. Eventually, I lay down and said that I now had to go to a clinic because I didn't know what to eat or what to think anymore.

But fortunately, it didn't come to that. The doctor explained to me that this was a typical reaction, as most people experience a phase of exhaustion after a sudden and strict dietary change. Switching to a new diet due to food intolerance is initially difficult, especially because you have to avoid many favorite foods, which can cause temporary frustration and have a negative impact on mental well-being.

The loving support of my family and friends helped me to navigate this transition phase, and gradually, I was able to recover.

7. Free From Panic Attacks After 15 Years

And it was true: Eliminating gluten and histamine had an effect, and the panic attacks became less frequent!

Finally, after three weeks, all gluten had been eliminated from my body, histamine levels were back to "normal," and I was free from panic attacks! There followed more days without panic attacks and without feelings of anxiety. Apart from the dietary changes, it was a truly "normal" life, after 15 years!

In the realm of calm, where silence sings,
A tone that resonates for me alone,
Panic attacks, a somber sound,
Now conquered, my heart's song resounds.

Days with low histamine, a delicate dance,
In gluten-free radiance.
My path woven from strength and light,
An ode to the liberated face.

Sara Mueller

1. The Search for a Food List

The intensive exploration of histamine intolerance and gluten sensitivity led me to the frustrating realization that I couldn't find a list of foods covering both aspects. While there were many good lists for low-histamine foods and gluten-free options, a list that met both requirements and covered the intersection simply didn't seem to exist! Even consulting a nutritionist confirmed my finding. Why this was the case was not clear to me or the nutritionist.

So, I embarked on a journey to create my own list of foods that were both gluten-free and low in histamine. This list was based on the intersection of common gluten-free and low-histamine food lists. You can find this comprehensive list starting from page 97.

2. The Supermarket Odyssey

Armed with my self-created food list, I ventured into the supermarket to buy some supplies. Shopping turned into an exhausting four-and-a-half-hour nightmare. In the produce section, I automatically reached for tomatoes, but had to put half of them back since tomatoes were not suitable for me. According to my list, tomatoes are histamine liberators. Among my favorite vegetables, zucchini and eggplant, I had to skip the eggplant due to its histamine content. Lemons, pineapples, bananas, and oranges were removed from my shopping basket and ended up in the shopping cart for my husband and daughter instead.

Then I reached the bakery section. I searched the back of gluten-free breads for low-histamine ingredients. They either contained yeast, locust bean gum, guar gum, or vinegar. I couldn't find any bread suitable for me. I decided to tackle the issue of bread substitutes later.

In the beverage section, I realized I could only go to the "tea section," as everything else - alcohol, coffee, or soft drinks - was out. The fine herbal tea blends contained either lemon, orange peel, nettle, or chamomile. I was overwhelmed with frustration at everything I had to avoid.

In the meat section, it got really "fun". No ground, sliced, smoked, or packaged meats, nor any sausages or cold cuts. That left me with no choice but to go to the fresh meat section and ask for a completely fresh chicken breast. Luckily, they had it, though it wasn't exactly cheap.

Shopping with a list of possible foods had miserably failed. I decided to buy what little I had found for myself and figure out a better way at home to manage my diet.

3. New Approach to Dietary Change

So, simply going shopping with a list of possible foods was not the right approach. The "bans" were too extensive, and replacement products were hard to find, at least not in a regular supermarket.

Moreover, a fundamental challenge arose: I had to cook both low-histamine, gluten-free meals for myself and normal meals for my family. Therefore, I changed my approach and developed a new five-step process.

First, I decided which recipes I wanted to prepare in the coming week.

In the second step, I divided each recipe into two categories: "regular" for my daughter and husband, and "low histamine" and "gluten-free" for myself. In the third step, I gathered the ingredients for each recipe and category. The ingredients for a "regular" recipe were easy to find and quickly added to my shopping list. Assembling the ingredients for "my recipe" took time as I had to carefully check each item against my list for histamine and gluten-containing components.

In the fourth and most time-consuming step, I searched for alternatives for these unsuitable ingredients. In the fifth step, I researched where I could buy these alternative foods. Many specifically low-histamine and gluten-free foods are not available in regular Swiss supermarkets. Instead, they must be sourced from health food stores, specialized shops, or even specialty stores in Germany or Italy.

I will explain my approach using the example recipe "Pasta with Pesto":

For the "regular recipe" category, the ingredient list includes pasta, store-bought pesto, and Parmesan cheese. This made the shopping list for this recipe easy to compile.

For the low histamine and gluten-free recipe category, I created the ingredient list as follows: Pasta, according to typical lists, is either gluten or histamine-containing. There are now numerous gluten-free pastas available. I had to be particularly cautious about histamine-containing ingredients, which ruled out varieties made from lentils, chickpeas, or buckwheat, leaving behind gluten-free options made from corn or rice.

Pesto: Store-bought pesto contains histamine. While seeking alternatives to store-bought pesto, I decided to prepare it myself. Therefore, I had to scrutinize the ingredients. For a simple pesto, these include basil, pine nuts, garlic, salt, Parmesan cheese, olive oil, and freshly ground pepper.

The problematic ingredients are: pine nuts (due to their histamine content), garlic (histamine), Parmesan cheese (histamine), regular salt (histamine), and pepper (histamine).

An appropriate alternative for pine nuts are macadamia nuts. I chose to omit garlic instead of replacing it. I already knew I needed iodine-free salt. It was impossible to replace Parmesan in the pesto, so I decided to forgo both Parmesan and pepper.

Cheese: In an online forum, I came across the suggestion to use mozzarella instead of Parmesan.

After researching, I was able to complete the shopping list with the ingredients for my personal recipe. In the final step, I had to find suitable shopping locations for all the groceries. Thanks to the internet, I could search efficiently. The "regular" pasta, ready-made pesto, Parmesan, macadamia nuts, mozzarella, and olive oil were available at the regular supermarket. I found gluten-free pasta made from corn and iodine-free salt at a health food store. Fresh basil, grown in a pot, I intended to buy at a nearby garden center.

This approach proved effective. On one hand, it gave me the feeling that despite my restrictions, I could still enjoy varied meals. On the other hand, it saved me from daily research into suitable recipes and their ingredients, as I could plan a week in advance. Thus, shopping became a positive experience again.

To help ease your first weeks of dietary adjustment, I've compiled a weekly plan with low-histamine and gluten-free recipes for you. You can find it and the corresponding recipes starting on page 111.

4. Obstacles

Here are some hurdles I encountered along the way. I share them with you so you can learn from my mistakes and save time. The path to dietary change requires a lot of time and presents several challenges. You can find more stumbling blocks and alternatives starting on page 93.

Stove Top: In the first weeks of my dietary transition, cooking felt like juggling in a circus. I juggled with six pots on only four stove burners. There was one pot for regular pasta, another for gluten-free and low-histamine pasta, one for tomato sauce, another for alternative tomato sauce, and of course, one for vegetables cooked in low-histamine and gluten-free broth, not to mention the frying pan for meat.

After a while, this juggling act became too cumbersome, and I decided to purchase two external camping stove burners from the camping department of a department store. This purchase significantly eased my work in the kitchen since I can now prepare everything simultaneously with six cooking surfaces.

Rice Cooker: It took me a while to find pasta that suited my taste. In the meantime, I settled for rice. Dealing with large quantities of rice, I was grateful for the Christmas gift from my brother-in-law and his wife: a rice cooker. This not only saves a stove burner but also simplifies rice preparation. Therefore, I highly recommend a rice cooker.

Medications: At this point, I already knew my body reacted sensitively to medications, so I usually took only half of the recommended dose. When I had severe headaches and wanted to take aspirin, I briefly researched online to ensure it was safe.

In doing so, I came across information that was previously unknown to me: Many medications contain ingredients that can release histamine or block the enzyme diamine oxidase (DAO).

The list of problematic ingredients was quite long. For example, anti-inflammatory pain relievers can increase histamine release, expectorants and analgesics can block the DAO enzyme. Surprisingly, medications like aspirin, mefenamic acid, metamizole, and morphine are among those that should be avoided with histamine intolerance.

The list of tolerated medications was rather limited, including ibuprofen and paracetamol. (SIGHI, Swiss Interest Group Histamine Intolerance, Medications, 2023)

Emergency Passport: Researching medications also made it clear to me that in case of emergency, doctors needed to be informed about which medications I could take and which I couldn't. Naturally, I also informed my husband and family about these new findings and emphasized that they must inform doctors about my specific needs in an emergency. Additionally, I created my own emergency passport, which I kept in the front of my wallet from then on.

5. Twelve Weeks Free From Panic Attacks!

Now that I had compiled a list, adjusted recipes, and started with the dietary changes, I realized how incredibly important it was to inform my family about my new dietary situation. This enabled us to develop a better understanding together for potential mood swings, as many challenges still lay ahead. It also allowed us to discuss our future meals, whether it meant preparing different dishes or agreeing on a common recipe.

In this way, I could address the upcoming challenges at any time, although I don't yet have a clear idea about them and would like to refrain from thinking about them for now. These include visits to restaurants and hotel stays. My husband and daughter have assured me of their unconditional support, whether it's with shopping or simply through their daily moral support.

And so, I had the first weeks behind me: 12 weeks free from panic attacks!

From then on, it was about experimenting, testing, observing, adding, and omitting. Since stress or other life circumstances can also promote histamine release, there may be times when you tolerate more or less histamine. Therefore, occasionally, you may also tolerate foods higher in histamine. This is very individual, and it's best to approach it gradually until you know your body well enough.

6. On the Way to a Low-Histamine and Gluten-Free Diet

1. Educate yourself thoroughly on both topics.
2. Compile your own list of gluten-free and low-histamine foods.
3. Inform your family, partner, or household that you will be changing your diet in the near future. Discuss how you want to cook - whether you want to prepare two different recipes or if everyone will follow your meal plan. This decision significantly influences cooking, pantry stocking, and shopping.
4. Also, ask them to motivate and support you daily with loving words, as it's not easy to change every meal.
5. Compile your favorite dishes and check against your list to see if they are low in histamine and gluten-free. If not, look for possible alternatives, such as using bell pepper sauce instead of tomato sauce.
6. Create a weekly meal plan and based on that, make your shopping list for the week.
7. Start with a fully gluten-free and low histamine diet from the first weeks.

8. Only after all symptoms have disappeared for a longer period, you can test new histamine-rich foods for tolerance.

7. Looking Back

Now, looking back over the past 45 years, I must say that if histamine intolerance and gluten sensitivity had been recognized earlier, serious consequences could have been avoided. With all this new knowledge, I see my life path and especially my medical history in a different light:

My likely inherent hypersensitivity and being a synesthete bring significant advantages, but of course, they also have negative aspects: there are too many external stimuli. This leads to stress and can affect the gut. For me, this manifested as nonspecific allergies, although no allergy test ever yielded results. Also, the unclassifiable asthma was a hint. Histamine can also cause asthma-like symptoms.

The many strong medications for pneumonia and asthma certainly did not help. On the contrary, in my youth, my histamine levels were probably overflowing daily without anyone noticing. My intolerance to alcohol should have raised questions as well. Today, I know that alcohol is one of the biggest histamine liberators.

Perhaps the abundant pasta consumption in Italy additionally contributed to gluten sensitivity, or maybe it was something else entirely. What is factual, though, is that histamine intolerance often doesn't come alone but rather brings along other food intolerances. Thus, signs of unrecognized histamine intolerance and gluten sensitivity could have been noticed years before I began experiencing panic attacks.

The abdominal cramps that followed and the numerous examinations that ultimately revealed nothing unusual were the next steps in the downward spiral of histamine intolerance and gluten sensitivity. I was considered healthy, but I wasn't.

As the permeability of the intestinal wall (Leaky Gut Syndrome) continued to increase, unwanted substances could enter the bloodstream. When the intestinal mucosa is disrupted and permeable as in Leaky Gut Syndrome, harmful substances can enter the bloodstream in greater quantities and ultimately reach the brain. In my case, these disruptions of the gut-brain axis were accompanied by psychological symptoms such as anxiety, dizziness, and panic attacks. Another disorder of the gut-brain axis could be irritable bowel syndrome. Medical experts believe that larger amounts of toxins crossing the blood-brain barrier over time can lead to it becoming "leaky" and more permeable. Leaky Brain means that the blood-brain barrier can no longer fully perform its protective function. This can repeatedly lead to mood swings, depression, and much more.

Leaky Gut promotes Leaky Brain.

And so came the time when panic attacks appeared in my life. From that point on, unfortunately, my symptoms were only considered from a purely psychological perspective. The connections with nutrition or even a holistic approach were neglected. It was only through meeting and being diagnosed by a new doctor that my attention shifted to histamine intolerance and gluten sensitivity. Subsequently, I should have paid more attention to histamine intolerance, not just gluten sensitivity. This realization might have enabled me to possibly prevent a "second round."

After analyzing my life story and medical history, it became clear to me that I have been suffering from histamine intolerance and gluten sensitivity for **at least 30 years!** Astonishingly, no doctor has ever made this diagnosis during all this time.

This insight not only gives me a new perspective on my past but also raises the question of why these specific health challenges remained undetected for so long. It prompts me to contemplate the potential impact on my quality of life and underscores the importance of a more thorough and holistic medical examination. Reflecting on my own history serves not only for self-reflection but also aims to emphasize the need for improved medical attention to rare or difficult-to-diagnose conditions.

8. My Wish

My wish is that in the future, no one else will have to go through the arduous path that I had to endure. That's why I am sharing my story publicly, to help as many people as possible—those struggling with panic attacks, those facing irritable bowel syndrome, or those with nonspecific allergies. I want to show where these problems can lead and what causes may lie behind them. It's important to recognize that panic attacks may not exclusively have a psychological origin.

> **You must be the change**
> **you wish to see in the world.**
> Mahatma Gandhi

It took courage to share my personal journey, but I've written this biographical guide specifically for you. There are numerous people out there struggling with panic attacks who never talk about it. Let's face this taboo together and speak openly about it!

My goal is to raise awareness about issues like panic attacks and intolerances. I want to emphasize that there is, for example, a connection between irritable bowel syndrome and panic attacks. There are early warning signs to watch out for, such as unexplained abdominal cramps or intolerance to alcohol.

During my extensive research on histamine intolerance and gluten sensitivity, I fell into several dietary traps. I want to spare you from these experiences and provide concrete insights into how adjusting your diet can alleviate symptoms and possibly make them disappear.

In short, my aim is to show you ways to take shortcuts on your own path. Life can be so colorful and fulfilling. I hope my experiences can help you along the way.

INFORMATION AND KNOWLEDGE

THE CONNECTION BETWEEN GUT, BRAIN, AND PSYCHE

In order to understand better the body, we should first familiarize ourselves with some fundamental concepts. Some of these are already well-researched, while others, such as neurogastroenterology, is still in his infancy. This discipline examines how the nervous system interacts with the gastrointestinal tract. Scientists agree that the gut has a greater influence on our health, emotions, and thoughts than we previously knew.

The communication between the gut and the nervous system is a complex and constantly changing system. Nerves, hormones, and the immune system all play a role. It is important to note that the relationship between the gut and the brain is influenced by many factors, including genetic predispositions, diet, and lifestyle.

The connection between the gut and the brain is often referred to as the "brain-gut axis" or "gut-brain axis" and describes the complex interaction between the digestive system (gastrointestinal tract) and the brain. The "gut-brain axis" is like a telephone line between the abdomen and the boss, the brain. This telephone line consists of a complex connection of nerves, hormones, and the immune system of the gut, which communicate with the central nervous system (brain and spinal cord). It is a bidirectional communication, meaning signals can be sent both from the brain to the gut and vice versa.

The idea behind this is that the abdomen and brain are strongly interconnected. When the abdomen is not well, it can also upset the brain, and vice versa. The condition of the abdomen can even affect feelings and thoughts.

Research has shown that the abdomen can send many messages to the brain, which can then influence mood, behavior, and even thinking.

On the other hand, the brain can influence the gut through the autonomic nervous system, affecting functions such as digestion and blood flow. The vagus nerve plays a crucial role in the communication between the central nervous system (brain) and the so-called enteric nervous system (ENS).

The connection between the vagus nerve and the ENS is a good example of the "brain-gut axis." The vagus nerve transmits signals between the brain and the gastrointestinal tract. This transmission of information occurs in both directions; for example, the brain can respond to changes in the digestive system, and conversely, the ENS can send signals to the brain. Overall, the connection between the vagus nerve, the ENS, and the brain demonstrates how closely the different parts of the nervous system are interconnected and how they work together to regulate the body's functions.

Stress, emotions, and food can influence the conversation between the gut and the brain. Examples of interactions and their effects include:

1. Neurotransmitters: The gut produces a significant amount of neurotransmitters, particularly serotonin. Serotonin is an important chemical messenger in the brain that affects mood and well-being. Imbalances in the gut can therefore impact mood and emotional well-being.

2. Immune System: A large part of the immune system is located in the gut. When inflammation or problems occur in the gut, it can activate the immune system and trigger inflammatory responses throughout the body. These inflammations can affect the brain and cause neurological symptoms.

3. Hormones: The gut and the brain also communicate through hormones. For example, stress can affect the digestive system, and conversely, disrupted digestion can cause stress. Cortisol, known as the stress hormone, can influence gut function.

4. Stress Response: The gut can respond to stress by reducing blood flow and slowing down digestion. On the other hand, prolonged stress can also lead to digestive problems.

5. Microbiome: The gut has many tiny residents, such as bacteria and other microorganisms. These work together to digest food and produce important substances. Surprisingly, they can even communicate with the brain and influence it. If the gut team is not properly balanced, it could be linked to some problems in the head. Certain bacteria in the human gut help with digestion, extract vitamins from food, strengthen the immune system, and protect against pathogens. The gut team even influences metabolism, inflammation, and mental health.

1. The Nervous System

The nervous system consists of many billions of nerve cells, known as neurons. It orchestrates complex communication within the human body. There are about 100 billion of these neurons in the brain alone. Each nerve cell is made up of a body and various extensions. The shorter extensions, also called dendrites, act like antennas to receive signals from other nerve cells, for example. At the same time, the long extension, the axon, which can be over a meter long, transmits these signals further.

Central Nervous System (CNS) and Peripheral Nervous System (PNS): There are two types of nerve pathways in the body, the central nervous system (CNS) and the peripheral nervous system (PNS). The CNS, which includes the brain and spinal cord, is safely housed in the skull and spine. The PNS includes all other nerves in the body. There are sensory nerves that bring information from the senses to the CNS, and motor nerves that send signals from the CNS to the muscles. Thus, the PNS acts as a communication pathway between the CNS and the rest of the body.

Somatic Nervous System and Autonomic Nervous System: The somatic nervous system, also known as the voluntary nervous system, controls things that can be consciously controlled, such as facial muscles, arms, and legs. On the other hand, the autonomic nervous system, also known as the involuntary nervous system, regulates automatic body functions that cannot be consciously controlled, such as breathing or heartbeat. It is always active, receiving signals from the brain and sending them to the body. Conversely, it transmits information from the body to the brain, such as how fast the heart is beating. The autonomic nervous system can quickly adapt to different conditions. For example, when it is warm, it increases blood flow to the skin and makes you sweat to cool your body down.

The autonomic nervous system is further divided into three areas:
• Sympathetic nervous system
• Parasympathetic nervous system
• Enteric nervous system (ENS)

Enteric Nervous System (ENS), the "Second Brain": The enteric nervous system is also known as the "second brain" or "gut brain" because it is an independent nervous system in the digestive tract. This means it has the ability to function autonomously without constant control by the central nervous system (brain and spinal cord), although both systems do interact. However, 90% of the information flows from the ENS to the brain and only 10% in the opposite direction. With the discovery of the enteric nervous system (ENS), researchers came to the conviction that the brain is not the only "captain" on board the human body.

How the ENS is involved in the interactions between the gut and the brain and what potential dysregulations can lead to:

A. Communication with the Central Nervous System (CNS): Through the autonomic nervous system and the enteric nervous system, signals are sent to the central nervous system. This allows for communication between the gut and the brain. For example, when problems occur in the digestive tract, the ENS can send signals to the brain, leading to corresponding reactions such as nausea, abdominal pain, or changes in appetite.

B. Neurotransmitters: The ENS produces a variety of neurotransmitters, including serotonin, dopamine, and acetylcholine, which affect mood, well-being, and digestion. An imbalance of these neurotransmitters in the ENS can negatively impact mood, well-being, and digestion.

C. Influence on Gut Motility: The ENS regulates the muscle movements in the digestive tract that are necessary for digestion and the transport of food. When the ENS is disrupted, digestive problems such as constipation or diarrhea can occur.

D. Immune System and Inflammation: The ENS is closely connected with the immune system in the gut. It can regulate inflammatory responses that could otherwise spread to the brain and trigger neurological symptoms.

E. Stress Response: The ENS responds to stress by affecting digestion. Stress can activate the ENS and cause digestive problems, which in turn can affect well-being. Particularly sensitive individuals often react with stomach or bowel disturbances to stress or everyday problems. In such cases, dysregulations within the ENS occur, often referred to as irritable stomach or irritable bowel. (Mayer, 2019), (Paul Enck, 2019), (Schemann, 2020), (Zinser, 2023)

2. The Microbiome

Another factor that influences mental health is the microbiome. The microbiome consists of the various microorganisms in your body, such as bacteria, viruses, and fungi. In humans, it mainly refers to the diversity of organisms in the gastrointestinal tract. The composition of the microbiome is also influenced by factors such as stress, medication, and diet, which we can control. The gut microbiome can interact with signaling pathways that affect the brain, and vice versa. This communication between the gut microbiome and the brain occurs through various pathways, including:

1. Neuroendocrine Pathways: The microbiome can send signals to the brain via neurotransmitters like serotonin and dopamine, which influence mood and behavior regulation systems.

2. Immunological Pathways: The microbiome can affect the gut's immune system, which in turn regulates inflammatory processes and immune responses throughout the body, including those that can affect the brain.
3. Vagus Nerve: The vagus nerve serves as an important connection between the gut and the brain, allowing signals to be transmitted in both directions.
4. Metabolic Pathways: The microbiome can produce metabolites that enter the brain via the bloodstream and influence various functions.

Scientists are currently intensively researching the connection between gut bacteria and mental health. Studies show links between changes in the gut microbiome and mental disorders such as depression, anxiety, and neurological diseases. Research findings suggest that the gut microbiome is associated with a variety of physiological processes, including metabolic processes, hormone regulation, immune response, nervous system functions, muscle functions, and digestive processes. The microbiome protects the body from diseases, supports the immune system, and influences how people feel, think, and act. Therefore, a balanced gut microbiome is crucial for health.

3. Connection Between Diseases and the Nervous System

The human body is a complex system in which everything is interconnected and influences each other. When a person is in balance, they experience health and well-being. Even a slight imbalance can impair the body's ability to self-regulate. This can lead to a breakdown or dysfunction of various bodily processes, triggering a domino effect where further processes fall out of balance.

We experience various symptoms, for example:

- Stomach cramps
- Headaches
- Abdominal cramps
- Migraines
- Nausea
- Circulatory problems
- Diarrhea
- Dizziness
- Colic
- Skin rash

If we are honest, we know that most people in such a case turn to a conventional pill and hope that the unpleasant symptom will soon disappear. In some cases, the symptoms can worsen and lead to the following:

- Irritable bowel syndrome (IBS)
- Leaky gut syndrome
- Mental disorders such as depression or anxiety

Recent research findings reveal an impressive connection: As the severity of depression, anxiety, and other mental illnesses increases, the incidence of accompanying irritable bowel syndrome also rises. In cases of severe depression, 90% of those affected additionally suffer from irritable bowel syndrome.

1. Anxiety Disorders

Fear, as a natural defense mechanism, is deeply rooted in us. It once allowed humans to quickly flee from predators. The feeling of fear puts the body on high alert, prompting us to assess the danger of a situation and take appropriate defensive measures, whether it be fleeing, waiting, or attacking. Once the threatening situation is over, the fear dissipates.

When fears arise in "inappropriate" situations, where there is no actual danger, medical professionals refer to it as an anxiety disorder. In such cases, normal everyday situations are suddenly perceived as threatening. Anxiety disorders are categorized into those with a specific trigger (phobia), such as fear of people, spiders, or flying, and those without a specific trigger.

Anxiety disorders without a specific trigger include panic disorder and generalized anxiety disorder. Individuals with a panic disorder repeatedly experience sudden panic attacks without an identifiable cause. On the other hand, symptoms of generalized anxiety disorder persist continuously. People with generalized anxiety disorder are constantly driven by exaggerated fears, such as the worry that something might happen to loved ones. In Switzerland, approximately 15-20% of the population suffers from anxiety disorders. Women are twice as likely as men to develop an anxiety disorder (Universitätsspital, 2023).

But herein lies not only the opportunity for intervention but also the possibility of understanding and guiding the flow of thoughts and fears. Managing anxiety disorders is akin to the art of regaining control over one's mental network and steering thoughts in a positive direction. This requires practice, mindfulness, and often professional support. It is entirely possible to break the cycle and steer the flow of thoughts in a new, more positive direction.

Panic attacks serve in a way as signposts, a final "warning" before turning into a dead end. They are by no means "evil" but rather a signal from your body that an immediate course correction is necessary. Apparently, warning signs have been overlooked, ignored, or deliberately disregarded. In such moments, the body pulls the emergency brake with panic attacks. Your psyche or soul wants to make it clear that changes are needed. Neither your brain nor any other part of you is harmed in this moment; it is merely a safety measure.

2. Symptoms of a Panic Attack

Panic attacks are not uncommon. A panic attack strikes out of the blue; it is a phase of extreme fear. These fears lead to a normal physical and psychological alarm or flight reaction.

Possible symptoms include:
- Rapid heartbeat: The heart starts to beat quickly and irregularly, often accompanied by a noticeable pounding in the chest area.
- Shortness of breath or hyperventilation: Breathing becomes shallower and faster, leading to a feeling of breathlessness or the need to take deep breaths.
- Sweating: Intense sweating, even when it is not particularly warm, is a common sign.
- Trembling or shaking: Muscles may tremble or tense up in response to the heightened activation of the nervous system.
- Dizziness: Many people experience feelings of dizziness, lightheadedness, or unsteadiness.
- Nausea or stomach problems: The gastrointestinal tract is sensitive to stress, so nausea, stomach pain, or digestive issues may occur.
- Feelings of heat or cold: A sudden sensation of warmth or cold, regardless of the actual ambient temperature.
- Tingling or numbness: Tingling sensations or numbness can occur in the hands, feet, or other parts of the body

3. Course of a Panic Attack

A panic attack can occur suddenly and unexpectedly, without you having noticed any clear warning signs. In a very short time, your fear or panic can become overwhelming, leading to an intense feeling of despair. This fear may seem irrational and is often accompanied by thoughts that you are losing control, going insane, or dying.

Physically, a panic attack can manifest through various symptoms. Your heart may start to race or beat irregularly, accompanied by shortness of breath or the sensation of being unable to breathe. Trembling, sweating, dizziness, and lightheadedness are also typical, as well as nausea or stomach issues. You might also experience chest pain, numbness, tingling, or the feeling of being disconnected.

Mentally, a panic attack can make you feel like you are losing touch with reality or going crazy. Thoughts may arise that you are having a heart attack, stroke, or another life-threatening illness. The urge to flee the situation or retreat to a safe place is often very strong.

After a panic attack, you feel immensely exhausted, as the body is drained by the intense stress reaction. Often, this is followed by the fear of further attacks or worries about when and where the next one might occur.

4. Measures During Panic Attacks

1. Pause.
2. Control Your Breathing: Learn to breathe calmly, slowly, and deeply into your abdomen (abdominal breathing). Inhale and count to three, exhale slowly and count to five. This activates the parasympathetic nervous system, leading to a slowing of the heart rate.
3. Seek Distraction: Divert your attention by focusing on something else. This can be counting numbers or looking at a calming image.
4. Positive Self-Talk: Have loving compassion for yourself, such as:

"It's important that I love myself and treat myself with compassion, especially in challenging moments." Simply observe the emotions that arise without judging them.

5. Practice Mindfulness: Learn exercises that enhance physical and mental awareness.

5. Fear of Fear

The fear of fear occurs when someone constantly worries about becoming anxious and subsequently experiencing a panic attack. This can lead the person to avoid certain situations or activities to prevent anxiety symptoms, thus trying to maintain control. Sometimes, just the thought of potential symptoms can make the person anxious. This can make daily life challenging.

People suffering from the fear of fear live in a constant state of worry that a panic attack or extreme anxiety symptoms might occur. This worry can be so intense that it triggers a panic attack itself, creating a vicious cycle.

This type of fear can take various forms, including (Heike Alsleben, 2011; Bandelow et al., 2023):

1. Avoidance behavior: People avoid certain places, activities, or situations to minimize the likelihood of a panic attack.
2. Physical symptoms: The mere thought that anxiety symptoms might occur can already trigger physical symptoms like heart palpitations, sweating, or trembling.
3. Restricted lifestyle: Due to the fear of fear, people might severely limit their lives to avoid potential triggers (e.g., avoiding public transportation, not going to supermarkets, etc.).
4. Excessive control: An overwhelming need for control to ensure that nothing happens can also be a sign of the fear of fear.

6. What Helps Against Panic Attacks?

Panic attacks and the fear of them can cause significant distress and severely impact daily life. Countermeasures are varied: behavioral therapy, mindfulness techniques, breathing therapy, medications, etc. Another fascinating possibility is to consider the connection between the psyche and nutrition, as panic attacks are not always triggered solely by stress or psychological disorders but also by diet. Food intolerances such as histamine intolerance and gluten sensitivity ("HiGlu") can be potential triggers. Together with professionals, dietary adjustments can be made by keeping a food diary and conducting tests if necessary to determine if an intolerance is present and how it influences anxiety symptoms.

INCOMPATIBILITY, ALLERGY, AND INTOLERANCE

1. Allergy and Intolernace

There are countless studies showing the direct correlation between an unhealthy diet and the resulting troubled psyche. But what is a healthy diet? Nowadays, the variety of healthy foods is incredibly large. I think everyone has to form their own opinion on this. This book focuses on food intolerances. From a medical perspective, "intolerance" is an umbrella term for various adverse reactions of the body to foods. This includes both allergies and intolerances, but the bodily processes are very different. A food allergy causes the immune system to react to a specific food. Our immune system is always involved. In the case of food intolerance, the immune system is not affected. One either has it genetically (enzyme defect or similar) or acquires it due to life circumstances. A food intolerance is an adverse reaction to a specific food while it is being digested. (European Centre for Allergy Research Foundation, ECARF, 2023).

2. Worldwide Increase

The fact is that these food intolerances are increasing worldwide. According to surveys, up to 25% of the world's population suffers from a food intolerance (NSW Food Authority, "Allergy and Intolerance," 2023). There are several studies and reports that address food intolerances and allergies worldwide, but exact and consistent global statistics are difficult to find due to regional differences in data collection. Nevertheless, there are estimates for the most common types of food intolerances. Here is an overview of common food intolerances worldwide:

- 68% from lactose intolerance
- 1-6% (estimated) from gluten sensitivity

- 1-3% from fructose malabsorption
- 1-2% from histamine intolerance
- 1% from celiac disease

3. What`s Behind the Increase

There are various reasons why food intolerances have increased compared to the past:

A. Changed eating habits: Modern eating habits differ significantly from those of earlier times. Nowadays, many people eat more processed foods, sugar, artificial additives, and chemicals, which were not as widespread in the past. These changes can promote food intolerances.

B. Changed food composition: The composition of foods has changed over time. New breeds of plants and animals are intended to meet the needs of the growing population. This can lead to certain food components, to which people are sensitive, becoming more common in the diet.

C. Environmental Impacts: The use of pesticides, herbicides, and other chemicals in agriculture has increased. These substances can leave residues in food and potentially lead to intolerances.

D. Antibiotics and Hormones: Antibiotics and growth hormones are often used in animal husbandry to increase productivity. Residues of these substances are present in meat and dairy products and can cause intolerances in some people.

E. Genetic Predisposition: Some people have a genetic predisposition to certain food intolerances, regardless of their diet. This predisposition can be more pronounced due to modern eating habits.

It is important to note that food intolerances vary from person to person, and the causes are diverse.

Nowadays, we are aware that different types of intolerances can cause not only physical discomfort but also have significant impacts on mental health. The burdens and restrictions associated with food intolerances, environmental allergies, or other sensitivities often lead to emotional and mental challenges. Stress, anxiety, depression, or other psychological symptoms are the result when someone struggles with the consequences of their intolerance.

4. Histamine Intolerance and Gluten Sensitivity as Triggers for Panic Attacks

The triggers that lead to an imbalance in the body are often reduced to "stress" or "lifestyle habits," or one seeks answers together with a psychologist. It is not uncommon for psychotropic drugs or other medications to be used in such situations.I believe this approach is legitimate. The root problem is often not adequately addressed. For 15 years, I treated these superficial causes like stress and psychological issues, with the result that the panic attacks were still present. But everything changed the day a doctor recognized that food intolerances were the cause of my prolonged suffering. The previously undetected combination of histamine intolerance and gluten sensitivity (briefly "HiGlu") was the root of my panic attacks. That was a real aha moment.

HISTAMINE INTOLERANCE

1. Basics

Histamine intolerance is a metabolic disorder that can be either acquired or genetically predisposed. Histamine intolerance (HIT), formerly known as histaminosis, describes the exceeding of an individual's tolerance threshold for histamine, leading to an excessive burden of histamine in the body. Histamine itself is a biogenic amine.

One can imagine a barrel that can be filled with histamine up to a certain mark. As soon as the tolerance threshold for histamine is exceeded, symptoms occur. The intensity and duration of these symptoms depend on how much the barrel overflows. This can last for hours, days, or even just minutes (Halliwill, 2023; Briden, 2023; SIGHI, Swiss Interest Group Histamine Intolerance, 2023; Histaminikus, 2023).

The topic of histamine is highly individual. Tolerance varies greatly based on individual sensitivity and is also influenced by the amount consumed. Additionally, stress, hormones, and many other factors play an important role. Therefore, it is necessary to determine for oneself the amounts that can be tolerated.

2. The Role of Histamine in the Body

Histamine is an important substance in the body involved in various physiological processes. It is released by certain cells and plays a key role in the immune system. Histamine is known for its role in allergic reactions, as it can cause symptoms such as itching, swelling, and the feeling of tightness in the chest. Furthermore, histamine also has functions in the gastrointestinal tract, where it can stimulate the production of gastric acid. This is important for the digestion of food. Histamine also acts as a neurotransmitter in the central nervous system and is involved in regulating sleep, wakefulness, and appetite control.

3. Histamine Breakdown in the Body (DAO and HNMT)

Histamine breakdown in the body is primarily managed by two enzymes: diamine oxidase (DAO) and histamine N-methyltransferase (HNMT).

Diamine oxidase (DAO) plays a crucial role in the progression of histamine intolerance. It is predominantly produced in the mucosa of the small intestine and is responsible for metabolizing histamine in the body. Another essential enzyme involved in histamine breakdown is histamine N-methyltransferase (HNMT). While DAO is mainly active in and produced by the intestinal mucosa, HNMT functions in the liver, kidneys, bronchial mucosa, and central nervous system (Histaminta, 2023).

To ensure sufficient DAO production in histamine intolerance, it is crucial to supply the body with specific vitamins and minerals (such as vitamin C, vitamin B6, zinc, copper, manganese, etc.). These nutrients act as cofactors for enzymes and play a significant role in activating diamine oxidase (DAO) and histamine N-methyltransferase (HNMT).

4. Histamine Liberators

Histamine liberators are substances that promote the release of endogenous histamine from mast cells or other histamine-producing cells. Mast cells are immune cells that play a role in regulating allergic reactions and inflammation by releasing biologically active substances such as histamine.

These liberators can originate from various sources, including certain foods (such as strawberries, lemons, or tomatoes), other biogenic amines, additives like flavor enhancers, dyes, and preservatives, as well as certain medications. Additionally, stress, physical exertion, lack of sleep, heat, and intense emotions such as anxiety can also lead to histamine release.

5. Symptoms of Histamine Intolerance

Merely consuming foods with varying histamine levels, as well as substances that promote histamine release (histamine liberators) or inhibit histamine breakdown (diamine oxidase inhibitors), can lead to a variety of symptoms. Therefore, the same person may have no complaints one day when consuming tomato paste, while on another day, they may suffer severe symptoms of histamine excess.

Below are some of the possible symptoms:
- Sleep disturbances
- Inner restlessness
- Headaches
- Migraines
- Nasal congestion
- Sneezing
- Coughing
- Asthma
- Arrhythmias
- Dizziness
- Abdominal pain
- Diarrhea
- Constipation
- Psychological disorders such as depression or anxiety disorders
- Joint pain
- Skin eczema
- Skin redness

The range of symptoms can vary from nearly asymptomatic to mild discomfort and even lead to a histamine crisis. This crisis can resemble an anaphylactic shock.

6. Diagnosis of Histamine Intolerance

Diagnosing histamine intolerance can be challenging as there are no specific tests that definitively indicate it. Typically, diagnosis is based on several factors: firstly, a medical history where the doctor inquires about symptoms and any possible temporal relationship to the consumption of histamine-rich foods. Secondly, blood or urine tests can provide various clues, such as measuring diamine oxidase (DAO) levels, histamine levels, or assessing vitamin and mineral status (vitamin B6, vitamin C, zinc, copper, etc.).

The most reliable method is an elimination diet, where there is a temporary switch to a low-histamine diet accompanied by a food diary. This involves documenting both consumed foods and any resulting symptoms to identify potential correlations.

Two rules of thumb should be noted: (Histaminikus F. , 2023)
- The fewer foods tolerated, the more filled the histamine and inflammation barrel, thus potentially more "poisoned" the gut.
- The fewer foods tolerated, the more filled the stress reservoir in the brain.

7. Treatment of Histamine Intolerance

Treatment for histamine intolerance involves transitioning to a low-histamine diet. Afterward, individual tolerance to histamine-containing foods can be assessed by gradually increasing intake.

Additionally, supplements such as vitamin C, vitamin B6, magnesium, and copper can help lower histamine levels. Further supplements containing the enzyme diamine oxidase (DAO) may also support management.

This approach aims to manage symptoms effectively through dietary adjustments and targeted supplementation, tailored to each individual's tolerance and needs.

When histamine levels in the body become too high, individuals with histamine intolerance may experience a histamine attack. This is characterized by one or more intensified symptoms that impair bodily functions. If symptoms become unmanageable, emergency medical services should be contacted.

8. Immediate Measures for a Histamine Attack

1. Control Breathing: Learn to breathe slowly and deeply into the abdomen. Inhale counting to three, exhale slowly counting to five. This activates the parasympathetic nervous system, slowing heart rate.
2. Drink Water: Water helps flush histamine from the body.
3. Take Vitamin C: Supports histamine breakdown.
4. Take Zinc: Inhibits histamine release.
5. Take Antihistamines.
6. Rest if Possible: Rest allows the body to regenerate.

9. Low-Histamine Foods

Typical food lists for histamine intolerance categorize foods into **low-histamine** and **high-histamine** categories. Low-histamine foods include:
- Meat: unprocessed fresh or frozen meat
- Fish and Seafood: freshly caught or frozen fish (cod, trout, perch, bass)
- Dairy Products: butter, fresh cheese, milk, young Gouda, cottage cheese, mozzarella, cream
- Fruits: apples, apricots, pears, blueberries, currants, cherries, lychees, mangoes, nectarines, peaches, rhubarb, melons
- Vegetables: broccoli, all green salads, cucumbers, potatoes, carrots, cabbage, pumpkin, leeks, corn, pak choi, bell peppers, radishes, turnip, beetroot, asparagus, zucchini, onions
- Grains: corn, rice, millet, quinoa. Note that corn may contain lectins, more on this from page 103.

10. High-Histamine Foods

These are foods that either act as histamine liberators (substances that promote the release of histamine in the body), DAO inhibitors (inhibit the enzyme diamine oxidase), or naturally contain histamine.
- Meat: smoked, marinated, dried, or poorly stored meat
- Fish and seafood: shrimp, shellfish, mussels, sardines
- Dairy products: long-aged cheeses such as Emmental, Parmesan, processed cheese, or blue cheese
- Fruits: pineapples, avocados, bananas, strawberries, grapefruits, raspberries, kiwis, limes, mandarins, oranges, papayas, and lemons, as well as overripe fruit and canned fruit
- Vegetables: algae, eggplant, avocado, beans, peas, pickles, legumes (peas, beans, chickpeas, etc.), lentils, horseradish, olives, mushrooms, sauerkraut, soy (soybeans, soy flour, etc.), spinach, tofu, tomatoes
- Grains: wheat, wheat germ, rye, barley, buckwheat, malt
- Be cautious with bread mixes: guar gum and locust bean gum are histamine liberators.

For a detailed list, I recommend the "Low-Histamine Diet Factsheet" from the Swiss Interest Group Histamine Intolerance, SIGHI (www.histaminintoleranz.ch).

11. Other Factors Leading to Increased Histamine Levels

The following should be noted:
- Avoid fermentation products (e.g., alcohol, vinegar, yeast)
- Avoid foods kept warm for long periods or reheated foods
- Avoid preservatives, colorants, acidifiers, etc., please note the E-list (flavor enhancers, glutamate, yeast extract)
- Avoid canned, ready-to-eat, or semi-prepared products
- Use only fresh produce (especially fish and meat) and, if possible, avoid pre-packaged goods.

Other factors that can increase histamine levels include:

Environmental influences: These include very strong cold or heat, loud noises like busy streets, or strong odors such as those in intensely fragrant spice markets. People with histamine intolerance also react more sensitively to chemical substances such as cleaning and household products (detergents, dishwashing liquids, humidifiers, etc.). Another reason for the release of histamine in the body can be exercise. Depending on the intensity and duration, this can increase histamine levels. (Halliwill, National Library of Medicine, 2023), (SIGHI, Swiss Interest Group Histamine Intolerance, 2023)

Hormonal balance: An imbalance in the hormonal balance intensifies the symptoms or even triggers histamine intolerance. Researchers now know that symptoms of histamine intolerance worsen before and during menstruation. This is because the hormone estrogen weakens the enzyme DAO and, on the other hand, histamine stimulates the ovaries to produce more estrogen. A vicious cycle can occur. In contrast, the hormone progesterone inhibits the release of histamine from mast cells. Progesterone prevents estrogen dominance and is an antihistamine. (Briden, 2023), (Histaminikus, Histaminikus, 2023)

Medications: Great attention must be paid to medications. Many common medications are histamine liberators or DAO inhibitors. (SIGHI, Swiss Interest Group Histamine Intolerance, Medications, 2023)

High sensitivity (HSP = Highly Sensitive Person): Stress leads to the release of endogenous histamine. (Schauwecker, 2023) Highly sensitive people are more prone to histamine intolerance because the threshold for stimuli (stress) is lower in highly sensitive people, making them more sensitive to many things.

The microbiome: The microbiome in the gut can produce histamine when certain types of bacteria are present. Histamine is produced by certain types of bacteria in the gut as a byproduct of their metabolism. These bacteria can convert histidine, an amino acid, into histamine. Histamine produced in the gut can enter the bloodstream and have various effects on the body. If the microbiome is imbalanced, it can lead to excessive production of histamine, which can, in turn, cause a lot of discomfort.

1. Basics

In gluten sensitivity, there is an intolerance to gluten or other grain components without detectable changes in the intestinal mucosa and without allergic reactions or involvement of the immune system. (AAAAI, 2022)

Chemically, gluten consists of two protein groups, the glutelins and the prolamins, which are called glutenin and gliadin in wheat. This protein component in the grain is also referred to as glue protein, as it gives the dough its elastic structure in connection with water and ensures that the bread rises, giving it its special texture. Gluten is heat-stable and has the ability to act as a binder and extender. It is often used as an additive in processed foods to improve texture, moisture retention, and taste. Therefore, gluten is particularly important in the production of baked goods, bread, pizza, pasta, and sweets. (Biesiekierski, 2017)

2. The Difference Between Celiac Disease, Wheat Allergy, and Gluten Sensitivity

Gluten sensitivity, celiac disease, and wheat allergy all refer to adverse reactions of the body to wheat or gluten, but they are not the same. Gluten sensitivity and wheat allergy are not autoimmune diseases, whereas celiac disease is classified as an autoimmune disease.

Celiac disease: Celiac disease is an autoimmune disease where the immune system attacks ingested gluten. The resulting inflammation significantly impairs the structure and function of the intestinal mucosa. Celiac disease can typically be diagnosed through a blood test followed by an intestinal biopsy. Treatment requires a lifelong gluten-free diet. (Celiac Society, 2023), (aha!, 2023), (IQWiG, 2022), (Ford, 2023)

Wheat allergy: Wheat allergy is not an intolerance; it is an allergy. Unlike gluten sensitivity and celiac disease, wheat allergy is an immune reaction to all proteins in wheat, not just gluten. The immune system identifies wheat proteins as harmful, prompting the production of antibodies that, together with other immune system components, attack the wheat. This causes inflammation, triggering a cascade of reactions. Symptoms range from skin rashes and breathing difficulties to gastrointestinal issues and can be severe. Diagnosis involves a combination of clinical evaluations, lab tests, allergy skin tests, and an elimination diet. (aha!, 2023)

Gluten sensitivity: Since 1970, there have been reports of patients reacting to gluten despite not having celiac disease or a wheat allergy. This condition now has a specific name: non-celiac gluten sensitivity, or NCGS. The causes of gluten sensitivity are not yet fully understood. Various scientific studies exist, such as the GLU-TOX study in Italy. (Dr. Schär Institute, 2023), (Luca Elli, MDPI, 2023)

It is increasingly evident that there is a link between gluten sensitivity and symptoms such as depression, anxiety disorders, panic attacks, and burnout. In particular, admissions to psychiatric facilities have increased over the past year. (Koning, 2023) Symptoms of gluten sensitivity include:

- Abdominal pain
- Muscle and joint pain
- Diarrhea
- Numbness in the extremities, muscle contractions
- Irritable bowel syndrome
- Nausea
- Skin rashes: eczema, skin redness
- Bloating, flatulence
- Weight loss
- Depression
- Fatigue, weakness
- Anxiety disorders, panic attacks
- Headaches
- Burnout

(American Academy of Allergy, Asthma & Immunology, 2023), (MDPI, Evidence for the Presence of Non-Celiac Gluten Sensitivity in Patients with Functional Gastrointestinal Symptoms: Results from a Multicenter Randomized Double-Blind Placebo-Controlled Gluten

Challenge, 2023), (Benotmane, 2023), (Catassi, 2023), (Schumacher, 2017), (aha!, 2023), (Ford, 2023), (Zopf, 2023), (Heilpraktiker, 2023).

3. Diagnosis of Gluten Sensitivity

Since the symptoms are very diverse, a definitive diagnosis can only be secured through self-experimentation. Certain foods are omitted while keeping a food diary. If the symptoms then disappear and one feels better, it can be certain that one has gluten sensitivity. To be completely sure, one can then perform a provocation test. One intentionally consumes the foods that were not tolerated before and observes whether the symptoms return.

4. Immediate Measures for a Gluten Attack

In the English-speaking world, the term "gluten attack" is known. In German, the expression "gluten attack" is not commonly used and there is no official medical definition for it. I use the term here to make such an incident more understandable.

A gluten attack occurs when people with gluten sensitivity or celiac disease accidentally ingest gluten. Even the slightest traces of gluten can cause the body to rebel against the gluten protein about 30 minutes later. The symptoms of a gluten attack can include abdominal pain, diarrhea, nausea, fatigue, and other discomforts.

The immediate measures for a gluten attack are:
1. Emotional: It is important not to feel guilty or inferior if one accidentally consumes gluten. This can happen unintentionally, and it is crucial to alleviate the emotional pain.
2. Drink water: Drink plenty of water, as it helps flush and cleanse the body.
3. Rest if possible: Sleep allows the body to regenerate.

5. Treatment of Gluten Sensitivity – Gluten-Containing Grains

The treatment for gluten sensitivity primarily consists of a gluten-free diet. This means avoiding foods that contain gluten.

Gluten-containing grains are: (Medizin, 2023)
- Wheat
- Rye
- Barley
- Spelt
- Grünkern
- Triticale
- Khorasan wheat (Kamut)
- Einkorn
- Emmer

Special Case of Oats: Oats are naturally gluten-free. But oats can be contaminated with gluten because they are often grown in fields previously used for wheat or rye. They are harvested using the same equipment, and there is usually no cleaning done after harvesting. Additionally, oats are often processed in the same mills as other grains. Therefore, it is important to ensure that you only purchase oats labeled as "gluten-free."

Special Case of Corn: Corn is gluten-free, but it can potentially be problematic due to its lectin content. Lectins are proteins that plants produce to protect themselves from predators. Inflammation of the intestine caused by lectins can activate mast cells present in the intestine. These mast cells tend to overreact, releasing substances such as histamine into the body. The tolerance to corn varies individually and should be determined through personal experience.

6. Foods That Contain Gluten-Containing Grains

- Pasta
- Flakes
- Malt products
- Bran
- Grist
- Couscous
- Bulgur
- Ebly
- Bread
- Pastries
- Breadcrumbs
- Dumplings
- Noodles
- Cakes
- Cookies
- Waffles
- Seitan
- Udon noodles

7. Foods That Unexpectedly Contain Gluten

Gluten is found not only in typical grains but surprisingly also in many processed foods where grains may not be the primary ingredient, often used as a binder or additive.

- Frozen fruit with sweeteners, frozen vegetables with additives and/or binders
- Generally, all sweets can contain gluten (in the form of barley malt or flavors).
- Ovomaltine, beer (malt)
- Potato-based pasta such as gnocchi, Schupfnudeln or dumplings
- Yogurt with grains or cookies such as Bircher muesli
- Highly processed foods with many additives and preservatives, flavorings and enhancers, such as light products, canned goods, marinated vegetables, ready-made sauces thickened with flour, ketchup, mustard, soy sauces, and ready meals
- Foods that are seasoned, pickled, breaded, or kitchen- or table-ready, such as cooked ham or corned beef with jelly
- Cosmetics and dental care products may also contain gluten.

TIPS, RECIPES, FOOD LIST,
WEEKLY PLAN

TIPS

1. The Devil is in the Details

During my transition to a low-histamine and gluten-free diet, I encountered many stumbling blocks. I would like to share these experiences with you so that you can possibly learn from my mistakes. Additionally, I spent a lot of time searching for alternatives to my beloved foods. I hope to save you from this time loss.

2. Topic Bread

Only specialized bakeries offer gluten-free bread. Normal or organic bakeries typically do not offer such bread because a separate bakery is required to ensure that no gluten particles contaminate the gluten-free bread. In Switzerland, there are few specialized gluten-free shops.

Once you find such a bakery, the question arises as to whether the bread is also low in histamine. This depends on the additives used. Since gluten-free flour does not contain gluten protein, a thickening agent is needed to hold the bread together. Popular choices are locust bean gum and guar gum. They can release histamine and thus lead to reactions in the body. Since individual tolerance to histamine varies from person to person, one must determine whether one can tolerate bread with locust bean gum or guar gum. I currently do not tolerate it and had to look for alternatives.

3. Topic Jam

I have no experience with store-bought jam as I always made my own. I believed that it contained no undesirable ingredients. I discovered that the gelling sugar I used contained citric acid, which was not the best product for a low-histamine diet! In my search for gelling sugar without citric acid, I found that pectin is a well-tolerated alternative. So, I made my own jam using pectin-containing gelling sugar.

4. Topic Pasta

Pasta presents a significant challenge. Nowadays, there are many gluten-free pasta options available on the market. For pasta, one should avoid those made from lentils, buckwheat, or chickpeas due to their histamine content. Varieties made from rice and/or corn are low in histamine. Nevertheless, caution is advised as corn contains lectins that can cause issues for those with histamine intolerance and gluten sensitivity. Whether one tolerates corn or not needs to be determined individually.

Once you've decided on a low-histamine and gluten-free pasta, it's important to note that each manufacturer offers a different taste experience. It's recommended to try out various products to find your personal preference.

5. Topic Tomato Sauce

The search for the perfect sauce for pasta was even more challenging than finding the pasta itself, as all options with tomatoes and ground meat were excluded. After some time, I discovered "fake" tomato sauce. It uses red peppers instead of tomatoes. You can prepare them yourself and freeze them in portions afterward.

Since the foods for my diet need to be prepared with considerable time and effort, occasionally relying on a ready-made product makes my work easier. Here's my secret tip for a ready-made "fake" tomato sauce: "No!mato Sauce Organic" from Histaminikus. Grated cheese, which usually adds a delicate touch at the end, is replaced by some cubes of mozzarella.

6. Topic Salad Dressing

If you suffer from histamine intolerance, consuming vinegar as well as lemon juice is not allowed. A salad dressing without the characteristic acidic note is often less appealing in taste. As an alternative to vinegar, I use verjus. Whether one tolerates it should be tested individually. Verjus is the juice of green, not fully ripe grapes. In the Middle Ages, it held an indispensable place in the world of spices. Combined with a little olive oil and salt (ensuring the salt does not contain iodine), it creates a perfect salad dressing.

FOOD LIST

1. Preliminary Remark

This list of low-histamine and gluten-free foods is based on an overlap of common low-histamine and gluten-free food lists.

Please note that sensitivity to histamine can vary individually. Therefore, it is important to determine for yourself which foods are tolerable and where your personal threshold for discomfort lies.

My list is for information and inspiration purposes only. It does not replace professional dietary advice. I do not assume liability for any inaccuracies or omissions in the list. The use of this information is at your own risk.

2. My Low-Histamine and Gluten-Free Food List

The foods are carefully categorized into suitable and unsuitable categories. Each food item is assigned to one of the categories to allow for more precise management.

> **Category 0:** **Highly Suitable** (gluten-free and nearly low-histamine)
> Category 1: Moderately Suitable (gluten-free and low in histamine)
> *Category 2:* *Less Suitable* (contains gluten and/or moderate in histamine)
> *Category 3:* *Extremely Unsuitable* (contains high levels of gluten and/or histamine)

On stressful days, I limit myself to consuming a minimal amount of foods from Category 1 and prefer products from Category 0 whenever possible.

Basically:
1. Avoid fermentation and fermentation products (e.g., alcohol, vinegar, or yeast).
2. Avoid long-heated or reheated foods.
3. Thaw rapidly and use immediately; do not thaw slowly in the refrigerator.
4. Avoid preservatives, colorants, acidity regulators; refer to the E-list which can be downloaded from the internet (flavor enhancers, MSG, yeast extract).
5. Avoid canned, ready-made, or semi-prepared products (especially no yeast extract).
6. Prefer fresh products, especially for fish and meat. Avoid packaged products if possible.

FRUITS

Category 0 = Highly Suitable

- Apple
- Apricot
- Bilberry
- Blackberry
- Blackcurrant
- Blueberry
- Cherry
- Cranberry
- Currant
- Date
- Dragonfruit
- Elderberry
- Gooseberry
- Grape
- Lychee
- Melon
- Mirabelle
- Nectarine
- Passionfruit
- Peach
- Persimmon
- Pomegranate
- Prickly pear
- Quince
- Sour cherry
- Starfruit

Category 1 = Moderately Suitable

- Damson plum
- Fig
- Mango
- Pear
- Plum
- Rhubarb
- Rose hip
- Watermelon

Category 2 = Less Suitable

- Banana
- Grapefruit
- Guava
- Kiwi
- Papaya
- Pineapple
- Rambutan
- Raspberry
- Strawberry

Category 3 = Extremely Unsuitable

- Lemon
- Lime
- Mandarin
- Orange

 VEGETABLES

Category 0 = Highly Suitable
- Artichoke
- Asparagus
- Beetroot
- Bell pepper, red, yellow
- Broccoli
- Cabbage varieties
- Carrot
- Cauliflower
- Celery
- Chicory
- Chinese cabbage
- Cucumber
- Fennel
- Iceberg lettuce
- Lamb's lettuce (Corn salad)
- Pak Choi
- Parsnip
- Plantain
- Pumpkin
- Radish
- Red cabbage
- Salad, all green varieties
- Savoy cabbage
- Swiss chard
- Sweet potato
- Zucchini

Category 1 = Moderately Suitable
- Brussels sprouts
- Corn (note: lectins!)
- Garlic
- Kohlrabi
- Leek
- Onions, white
- Snow peas

Category 2 = Less Suitable
- Arugula
- Beans
- Eggplant
- Horseradish
- Lentils
- Lupins
- Olives
- Onion, red
- Peas
- Pickled vegetables
- Soy, e.g., soybean
- Tofu

Category 3 = Extremely Unsuitable
- Algae, e.g. Wakame
- Avocado
- Mushrooms
- Sauerkraut
- Spinach
- Tomato

MEAT

Category 0 = Highly Suitable

- Beef, Veal, fresh/frozen
- Chicken/Poultry, fresh/frozen
- Goat, fresh/frozen
- Lamb, fresh/frozen
- Ostrich, fresh/frozen
- Pork, fresh/frozen
- Turkey, fresh/frozen

Category 3 = Extremely Unsuitable

- Canned meat
- Cold cuts
- Cured meat
- Jerky
- Meatloaf
- Offal, e.g., liver
- Raw ham, ham
- Salami
- Sausage, e.g., Bratwurst
- Shredded meat
- Smoked meat

 # FISH

Category 0 = Highly Suitable

- Cod, fresh/ frozen
- Perch, fresh/ frozen
- Pollock, fresh/ frozen
- Sea Bass, fresh/ frozen
- Trout, fresh/ frozen
- Whitefish, fresh/ frozen
- Wild Salmon, fresh/ frozen

Category 3 = Extremely Unsuitable

- All canned fish
- Anchovies
- Crayfish
- Farmed Salmon
- Fish sauce
- Mussels
- Sardines
- Seafood
- Shrimp
- Tuna

DAIRY PRDOCTS, EGGS

Category 0 = Highly Suitable
- Butter
- Cottage cheese
- Cream
- Cream cheese
- Fresh milk, UHT, PAST
- Goat's milk
- Mascarpone
- Mozzarella
- Quark (curd cheese)
- Ricotta
- Sheep's milk
- Young Gouda

Category 1 = Moderately Suitable
- Crème fraîche
- Feta
- Junket
- Milk powder
- Oat or coconut-based
- Panir
- Skyr, see fruit list
- Sour cream
- Whole egg, egg white Cat. 2, egg yolk Cat. 0
- Yogurt, plant-based oat or coconut-based

Category 2 = Less Suitable
- Cheese preparations, e.g., fondue
- Gouda, aged
- Mold cheese, blue and white
- Processed cheese
- Soy or lupine-based products
- Yogurt, Greek
- Yogurt, plant-based soy or lupine-based

Category 3 = Extremely Unsuitable
- Aged cheese, hard cheese
- Aged cheese, semi-hard cheese
- Aged cheese, soft cheese

STARCH, GRAINS

Category 0 = Highly Suitable

- Amaranth
- Millet
- Oats, only gluten-free!
- Potatoes
- Quinoa
- Rice
- Rice noodles
- Sweet potato

Category 1 = Moderately Suitable

- Corn, caution: contains lectins!

Category 3 = Extremely Unsuitable

- Barley
- Buckwheat
- Bulgur
- Einkorn
- Emmer
- Guar gum
- Khorasan wheat (Kamut)
- Locust bean gum
- Malt
- Oats
- Rye
- Spelt
- Wheat

 # OIL

Category 0 = Highly Suitable

- Coconut oil
- Linseed oil
- Olive oil
- Pumpkin seed oil
- Rapeseed oil

Category 2 = Less Suitable

- Safflower oil
- Sunflower oil
- Walnut oil

VINEGAR

Category 1 = Moderately Suitable
- Branntweinessig (distilled vinegar)
- Verjus Royal

Category 2 = Less Suitable
- Apple cider vinegar

Category 3 = Extremely Unsuitable
- Balsamic vinegar
- Red wine vinegar
- White wine vinegar

 NUTS, KERNELS

Category 0 = Highly Suitable
- Brazil nut
- Coconut
- Macadamia nut
- Pecan nut
- Pumpkin seeds

Category 2 = Less Suitable
- Hazelnut
- Peanut
- Sunflower seeds

Category 1 = Moderately Suitable
- Almonds
- Cashew nut
- Sesame

Category 3 = Extremely Unsuitable
- Walnut

HERBS, SPICES

Category 0 = Highly Suitable
- Basil
- Cardamom
- Kaffir lime leaf
- Lemongrass
- Oregano
- Parsley
- Rosemary
- Sage
- Salt, iodine-free
- Summer savory

Category 2 = Less Suitable
- Clover
- Cumin
- Fenugreek
- Mustard
- Nettle
- Paprika spice
- Wild garlic

Category 1 = Moderately Suitable
- Chives
- Cinnamon
- Dill
- Ginger
- Mint
- Vanilla

Category 3 = Extremely Unsuitable
- Bouillon, beware of MSG!
- Chili
- Curry
- Fish sauce
- Flavor enhancers
- Pepper
- Salt, iodized
- Soy sauce
- Spicy spices

SWEETENERS, SWEET

Category 0 = Highly Suitable
- Agave syrup
- Cane sugar
- Coconut blossom sugar
- Date syrup
- Fructose
- Glucose
- Honey
- Maple syrup
- Molasses
- Rice syrup
- Stevia

Category 1 = Moderately Suitable
- Caramel
- Sugar, granulated sugar
- White chocolate

Category 2 = Less Suitable
- Artificial sweeteners, e.g., aspartame
- Brown and black chocolate
- Erythritol
- Isomalt
- Sorbitol
- Xylitol (birch sugar)

Category 3 = Extremely Unsuitable
- Malt sugar, maltitol, malt

 # VITAMINS, MINERALS, TRACE ELEMENTS

Category 0 = Highly Suitable
- Vitamin B6
- Vitamin C
- Vitamin E
- Zinc

Category 2 = Less Suitable
- Folic acid
- Licorice

Category 3 = Extremely Unsuitable
- Iodine
- Potassium iodate

BEVERAGES

Category 0 = Highly Suitable
- Elderflower syrup
- Juice, according to fruit list
- Tea, bay leaves
- Tea, chamomile
- Tea, cistus
- Tea, fennel
- Tea, hibiscus
- Tea, lemon balm
- Tea, linden flowers
- Tea, moringa
- Tea, rooibos
- Tea, sage
- Tea, thyme
- Tea, tulsi
- Tea, verbena
- Water

Category 2 = Less Suitable
- Carbonated water
- Ovomaltine, cocoa
- Tea, black tea
- Tea, fruit
- Tea, green tea
- Tea, nettle
- Tea, rose hips

Category 1 = Moderately Suitable
- Decaffeinated coffee
- Milk
- Rice milk
- Tea, ginger
- Tea, lady's mantle
- Tea, Mint

Category 3 = Extremely Unsuitable
- Alcohol, e.g., wine, spirits
- Beer
- Cereal coffee
- Coffee
- Energy drinks
- Juice, orange juice
- Juice, tomato juice
- Soft drinks
- Soy milk

FOOD ADDITIVES

Attached are the most important food additives for me (colorants, pre-servatives,acidity regulators, flavor enhancers, sweeteners, thickeners, leavening agents, and flavorings. For a detailed list of histamine-con-taining additives (e.g., all E-numbers), I recommend the Food Compa-tibility List of the Swiss Interest Group for Histamine Intolerance (SIG-HI), as of 8/2023.

Category 1 = Moderately Suitable
- Baking soda
- Cream of tartar
- E 160a – Carotenes
- E 261 – Potassium acetate
- E 300 – Ascorbic acid, Vitamin C
- E 504 – Magnesium carbo-nate
- E 650 – Zinc acetate
- Pectin
- Potato/corn starch
- Vanilla sugar
- Weinstein baking powder

Category 2 = Less Suitable
- Agar-agar
- Aspartame
- Baking powder
- Citric acid
- Emulsifiers (all)
- Flavors
- Gelatin
- Glutamic acid/glutamates
- Preservatives
- Stabilizers (all)
- Yeast
- Acidity regulators

Category 3 = Extremely Unsuitable
- E 104 – Quinoline yellow
- Various colorants

WEEKLY MENU PLAN

low-histamine and gluten-free

MONDAY

| Sticky Rice with mango | Pasta with "fake" tomato sauce | Potatoes with crème fraîche dip and green salad |

TUESDAY

| Oatmeal with blueberries | Asian chicken pan with rice | Omelet with sour cherry filling |

WEDNESDAY

| Oat rolls | Trout fillet with herb butter, fried potatoes, and cauliflower | Pasta with pesto |

THURSDAY

| Cucumber cottage cheese crispbread | Beef Slices à la Minute with herb butter, rice, and broccoli | Baked sweet potato and zucchini slices with quark dip |

FRYDAY

| Oatmeal with persimmon | Chicken breast with pasta, romanesco, and cream sauce | Corn-couscous vegetable pan |

SATURDAY

| Oatmeal with blueberries | Pasta with "fake" tomato sauce
Baked apple with crispy filling | Sticky Rice with mango |

SUNDAY

| Oat rolls | Asian chicken pan with rice
Gluten-free cheesecake without crust | Pasta with pesto |

| BREAKFAST | LUNCH | DINNER |

RECIPES

This compilation of low-histamine and gluten-free recipes is based on my own creations as well as common recipes where I have replaced histamine and gluten-containing ingredients with suitable alternatives.

Please note that sensitivity to histamine can vary individually. Therefore, it's important to determine which foods are tolerable for you and to understand your individual tolerance levels.

Low-histamine and gluten-free recipes from the weekly menu plan:

- Sticky Rice with Mango
- Oatmeal with Blueberries
- Oat Rolls
- Cucumber Cottage Cheese Crispbread
- Oatmeal with Persimmon
- Pasta with "Fake" Tomato Sauce
- Potatoes with Crème Fraîche Dip and Green Salad
- Asian Chicken Pan with Rice
- Omelette with Sour Cherry Filling
- Trout Fillet with Herb Butter, Roasted Potatoes, and Cauliflower
- Pasta with Pesto
- Beef Slices à la Minute with Herb Butter, Rice, and Broccoli
- Baked Sweet Potato and Zucchini Slices with Quark Dip
- Chicken Breast with Pasta, Romanesco, and Cream Sauce
- Corn Couscous Vegetable Pan
- Baked Apple with Crispy Filling
- Gluten-Free Cheesecake without Crust

STICKY RICE WITH MANGO

Breakfast Lunch Dessert **Dinner**

For 1 person
Preparation time: 45 minutes

INGREDIENTS

- 1 rice cup (ca. 180 ml) sticky rice
- Water for rice cooker (see notes on page 148)
- 125 ml coconut milk
- 10 g sugar
- Pinch of salt (iodine-free)
- ½ mango

INSTRUCTIONS

1. Rinse sticky rice thoroughly under cold water, then place it in the rice cooker with the appropriate amount of water. Start the cooking program.
2. Gently warm for 3-5 minutes, but do not boil, coconut milk in a pot, stirring to dissolve sugar and a pinch of salt.
3. Once sticky rice is cooked, stir in the coconut milk-sugar mixture. Cover and leave it for 10 minutes until the rice absorbs the liquid.
4. Wash the mango thoroughly to ensure it is free from dirt.
5. Peel the mango.
6. Carefully cut the mango flesh, avoiding the seed. Cut mango into bite-sized thin or thick strips.
7. Serve sticky rice on a plate, arrange mango slices alongside, and enjoy.

OATMEAL WITH BLUEBERRIES

Breakfast   Lunch   Dessert   Dinner

For 1 person
Preparation time: 10 minutes

INGREDIENTS

- 250 ml water
- Pinch of salt (iodine-free)
- ⅓ tsp cinnamon (Note: Cinnamon may not be suitable for everyone)
- 40 g gluten-free rolled oats
- 100 g fresh blueberries
- 2 tsp maple syrup or an alternative (honey or agave syrup)

INSTRUCTIONS

1. Bring the water to a boil in a medium-sized pot with the salt, cinnamon, and rolled oats. Reduce the heat and let it simmer for about 5 minutes, stirring constantly, until a smooth oatmeal forms
2. Let the oatmeal sit for 3 minutes.
3. Transfer the oatmeal to a bowl.
4. Spread blueberries over the oatmeal and sweeten to taste with maple syrup.
5. Enjoy your meal!

Tip: During summer, I always buy fresh blueberries. I portion larger quantities and freeze them for later use, allowing me to enjoy these delicious berries even in winter months. To prevent extended thawing, especially important for those with histamine intolerance, I add the frozen berries directly to the water and oats mixture and let everything simmer together.

OAT ROLLS

Breakfast Lunch Dessert Dinner

For 1 person
Preparation time: 40 minutes

INGREDIENTS

- 2 medium carrots
- 100 g gluten-free rolled oats
- 3 tsp baking powder
- ½ tsp salt (iodine-free)
- 150 g quark (curd cheese)
- 1 egg

INSTRUCTIONS

1. Preheat the oven to 180°C / 356°F.
2. Peel and wash the carrots using a vegetable peeler, then grate them into a bowl using a box grater.
3. Mix the dry ingredients (rolled oats, baking powder, and salt) into the grated carrots.
4. In a separate bowl, combine the quark and egg until well mixed.
5. Stir the quark-egg mixture into the dry ingredients until a uniform dough forms.
6. With damp hands, shape the dough into 3-4 small buns and place them on a baking tray lined with parchment paper.
7. Bake the buns for about 30 minutes until golden brown, then let them cool.

Tip: For those with histamine intolerance and gluten sensitivity, nearly 95% of common bread products are unsuitable. Many flours contain gluten, and alternative binders like guar gum or locust bean gum are not suitable due to histamine content. It took me some time to find a recipe that circumvents both issues. I now enjoy these delicious oat buns almost daily. I typically make a double batch and freeze the extras.

CUCUMBER COTTAGE CHEESE CRISPBREAD

Breakfast   Lunch   Dessert   Dinner

For 1 person
Preparation time: 5 minutes

INGREDIENTS

- ¼ cucumber
- 1 slice of low-histamine, gluten-free crispbread (see notes on page 148)
- Approximately 100 g cottage cheese
- Fresh parsley for garnish

INSTRUCTIONS

1. Wash the cucumber and slice it thinly.
2. Spread the crispbread with cottage cheese.
3. Artfully arrange the cucumber slices on top of the cottage cheese.
4. Garnish with fresh parsley.

OATMEAL WITH PERSIMMON

Breakfast   Lunch   Dessert   **Dinner**

For 1 person
Preparation time: 10 minutes

INGREDIENTS

- 250 ml Water
- Pinch of salt (iodine-free)
- ⅓ tsp Cinnamon (Note: Cinnamon may not be suitable for everyone)
- 40 g Gluten-free rolled oats
- ½ fresh Persimmon
- Butter for frying
- 2 tsp Quark (or substitute yogurt)
- 2 tsp Maple syrup or alternative (honey or agave syrup)

INSTRUCTIONS

1. Bring water to a boil in a medium saucepan. Add salt, cinnamon, and gluten-free rolled oats. Reduce heat and simmer, stirring constantly, until a smooth oatmeal forms.
2. Transfer the oatmeal to a bowl and leave it to rest.
3. Wash the persimmon, remove the stem, and halve it. Slice one half into 3-4 mm thick slices.
4. In a large frying pan, melt a little butter over medium heat. Gently fry the persimmon slices until golden brown.
5. Arrange the fried persimmon slices over the oatmeal.
6. Add 2 tsp of quark (or yogurt) on top. Sweeten with maple syrup to taste.

PASTA WITH "FAKE" TOMATO SAUCE

Breakfast   **Lunch**   Dessert   **Dinner**

For 1 person
Preparation time: 50 minutes

INGREDIENTS

Sauce
- 3 red bell peppers
- 2 tbsp olive oil
- 1 tbsp low-histamine and gluten-free vegetable broth
- Pinch of salt (iodine-free)
- 1 tsp dried oregano
- ½ bunch fresh basil

Pasta
- 1 liter water
- Pinch of salt (iodine-free)
- 125 g low-histamine and gluten-free pasta (see notes on page 148)
- Cheese Substitute
- ½ package small mozzarella balls

INSTRUCTIONS

1. Preheat the oven to 220°C / 428°F.
2. Wash the bell peppers, halve them, remove the stems and seeds. Place them cut side down on a baking tray lined with parchment paper. Roast in the middle of the oven for 15 minutes or until the skin is almost blackened.
3. Transfer the roasted bell peppers directly into a plastic bag. Seal the bag and let them cool for 15 minutes.
4. Peel off the skins of the bell peppers using a sharp knife, then puree the flesh in a blender.
5. Wash the basil, remove the stems, finely chop the leaves, and set aside 3-4 leaves for garnish.
6. Heat the olive oil in a large frying pan and add the pureed bell peppers. Stir in the vegetable broth, salt, dried oregano, and chopped basil. Bring the sauce to a brief boil.
7. In a large pot, bring water and a pinch of salt to a boil. Cook the pasta until al dente according to package instructions.

Continued on next page

8. Place the pasta in the center of a serving dish and generously spoon the "fake" tomato sauce over it.
9. Garnish with mozzarella balls as a substitute for grated cheese. Decorate with reserved basil leaves according to taste.

Space for notes

After enjoying a dish, please note how well you tolerated it. If you noticed any intolerances or unpleasant reactions, also record these.

If you particularly liked a recipe, feel free to mark it and jot down your opinions.

If you made variations to the ingredients, make sure to note your adjustments.

POTATOES WITH CRÈME FRAÎCHE DIP AND GREEN SALAD

Breakfast   **Lunch**   Dessert   **Dinner**

For 1 person
Preparation time: 45 minutes

INGREDIENTS

Potatoes
- 100-150 g potatoes
- Approximately 1 liter water
- Pinch of salt (iodine-free)

Crème Fraîche Dip
- ½ cup crème fraîche
- ½ bunch chives or parsley
- Pinch of salt (iodine-free)

Salad with Dressing
- 1 portion salad
- 1 tsp low-histamine and gluten-free vegetable broth
- 1 tbsp lukewarm water
- 1 tbsp Verjus (vinegar substitute)
- 2 tbsp olive oil
- Pinch of salt (iodine-free)

INSTRUCTIONS

1. Wash potatoes thoroughly under cold water. Place them with skins on in boiling salted water and cook for about 20-30 minutes until they are tender but still firm.

2. Dip: Rinse and pat dry chives, then finely chop. In a small bowl, mix crème fraîche with a pinch of salt and chopped chives.

3. Wash salad and cut into bite-sized pieces. For the dressing, dissolve vegetable broth in lukewarm water, add Verjus, olive oil, and a pinch of salt. Stir well and mix with green salad.

4. Arrange the salad with dressing on one side of a plate, and on the other side, serve potatoes with dip.

ASIAN CHICKEN PAN WITH RICE

Breakfast   **Lunch**   Dessert   **Dinner**

For 1 person
Preparation time: 55 minutes

INGREDIENTS

Rice in Rice Cooker
(see notes on page 148)
- Water for rice cooker
- 1 rice cup Jasmine rice
  (about 180 ml)

Chicken Pan
- ½ white onion
- 1-2 kaffir lime leaves
- ½ pak choi (Chinese cabbage)
- 1 fresh chicken breast
  (see notes on page 148)
- Some olive oil
- 1 tsp vegetable broth with
  100 ml water
- 1 can coconut milk
  (250 ml)
- 2 tbsp Coco Aminos seasoning sauce (low-histamine soy substitute)
- Pinch of salt (iodine-free)

INSTRUCTIONS

1. Rinse rice thoroughly under cold water and then add to the rice cooker along with the specified amount of water. Start the cooking program.
2. Peel and finely chop the onion. Finely slice the kaffir lime leaves. Wash the pak choi thoroughly, halve it, and cut into strips. Cut the chicken breast into bite-sized pieces.
3. Heat oil in a frying pan and sauté the onion over medium heat until translucent. Add chicken pieces, briefly brown them, and deglaze with vegetable broth.
4. Reduce heat and add kaffir lime leaves and pak choi to the frying pan. Pour in coconut milk and Coco Aminos seasoning sauce, stir well, and let simmer for 15 minutes.
5. Serve rice in one bowl and the chicken pan in another bowl.

OMELETTE WITH SOUR CHERRY FILLING

Breakfast   Lunch   Dessert   Dinner

For 1 person
Preparation time: 50 minutes

INGREDIENTS

Omelet
- 60 g low-histamine and gluten-free flour (see notes on page 148)
- Pinch of salt (iodine-free)
- 120 ml milk
- 1 egg
- Butter for frying
- Some sugar and cinnamon (note: cinnamon may not be suitable for everyone)

Filling
- 150 g frozen sour cherries
- Some maple syrup

INSTRUCTIONS

1. In one bowl, mix flour and salt. In another bowl, whisk together milk and egg.
2. Fold the mixture into the dry ingredients, stirring until a smooth batter forms.
3. Let the batter rest in the refrigerator for about 30 minutes.
4. Preheat the oven to 60°C / 140°F.
5. Heat the sour cherries in a pot and mix with some maple syrup.
6. Heat a frying pan with some butter. Pour a portion of the batter into the pan and spread it thinly. Reduce the heat.
7. Once the omelet easily releases from the bottom of the pan, carefully flip it and fry until golden brown. Transfer to a plate and keep warm in the preheated oven. Repeat with the remaining batter.
8. Serve the omelet with the sour cherry filling and sprinkle with some sugar and cinnamon.

TROUT FILLET WITH HERB BUTTER, ROASTED POTATOES, AND CAULIFLOWER

Breakfast   **Lunch**   Dessert   **Dinner**

For 1 person
Preparation time: 40 minutes

INGREDIENTS
- 40 g butter
- ½ bunch fresh basil
- ½ bunch fresh parsley
- ¼ tsp dried oregano
- ¼ tsp dried thyme
- ¼ tsp dried rosemary
- Pinch of salt (iodine-free)
- 150 g potatoes (three medium-sized potatoes)
- Some olive oil
- About 200 g cauliflower
- Some salt (iodine-free)
- 150-200 g fresh trout fillet, e.g., rainbow trout

INSTRUCTIONS

1. Herb Butter: Allow butter to soften in a bowl. Wash and finely chop basil and parsley. Add chopped herbs (basil, parsley), dried oregano, dried thyme, dried rosemary, and a pinch of salt to the butter. Mix well and chill in the refrigerator.

2. Fried Potatoes: Wash potatoes, dice them, and fry in oil for 5 minutes. Cover and simmer over medium heat for 15-20 minutes or until soft. Season with salt before serving.

3. Cauliflower: Remove green leaves and core from the cauliflower, cut into florets, wash, and boil in salted water for 8-15 minutes until tender.

4. Trout Fillet: Heat herb butter in a frying pan, briefly fry trout fillet on both sides until cooked through.

5. Arrange everything on a plate and garnish with remaining herb butter.

PASTA WITH PESTO

Breakfast   **Lunch**   Dessert   **Dinner**

For 1 person
Preparation time: 30 minutes

INGREDIENTS

- Pesto
  (see notes on page 148)
- 100 g basil
- 10 g macadamia nuts
- 40 ml olive oil
- Some herbal salt
- 1 liter water
- Pinch of salt (iodine-free)
- 125 g low-histamine and
  gluten-free pasta
- Grated Cheese Substitute
- ½ pack small mozzarella
  balls

INSTRUCTIONS

1. Roughly chop macadamia nuts.
2. Wash basil, shake dry, and pluck the
   leaves. Set aside 3-4 leaves for deco-
   ration.
3. Blend basil, macadamia nuts, olive
   oil, and herbal salt in a food pro-
   cessor until smooth, creating pesto.
4. Cook pasta al dente according to
   package instructions.
5. Arrange the pasta on a plate and
   spread pesto over it. Distribute mozzarella balls evenly on top.
6. Garnish with fresh basil leaves as desired.

Tip: During summer when basil is abundant, make multiple portions
of pesto and freeze it.

BEEF SLICES À LA MINUTE
WITH HERB BUTTER, RICE, AND BROCCOLI

Breakfast   Lunch   Dessert   Dinner

For 1 person
Preparation time: 40 minutes

INGREDIENTS

Herb Butter
- 40 g soft butter
- ½ bunch fresh basil
- ½ bunch fresh parsley
- ¼ tsp dried oregano
- ¼ tsp dried thyme
- ¼ tsp dried rosemary
- Pinch of salt (iodine-free)

Stovetop Rice
- 300 ml water
- 100 g long-grain rice
- Pinch of salt (iodine-free)

Broccoli and Beef
- About 200 g broccoli
- 250 ml water
- Pinch of salt (iodine-free)
- Some olive oil
- 1 fresh minute steak
  (beef slice)

INSTRUCTIONS

1. Herb Butter: Allow butter to soften in a bowl. Wash and finely chop basil and parsley. Add herbs (basil, parsley, oregano, thyme, rosemary) and salt to the butter, mix well, and chill in the refrigerator.

2. Rice: Bring water to a boil, add a small amount of salt, and rice. Reduce heat, cover, and simmer for about 15-20 minutes until rice is al dente.

3. Broccoli: Wash broccoli, divide into florets, peel and chop the stalk. Bring water to a boil, add salt, and cook broccoli for about 5 minutes.

4. Beef: Heat oil in a frying pan. On high heat, briefly brown the minute steak on both sides.

5. Serve: Arrange minute steak, rice, and broccoli on a plate. Garnish with herb butter.

BAKED SWEET POTATO AND
ZUCCHINI SLICES WITH QUARK DIP

Breakfast **Lunch** Dessert **Dinner**

For 1 person
Preparation time: 40 minutes

INGREDIENTS

- 100 g sweet potatoes
- 1 medium zucchini
- About 2 tbsp olive oil
- 1 piece of fresh ginger (about 2 cm)
- Pinch of salt (iodine-free)
- About 70 g quark (curd cheese)
- ½ bunch fresh parsley

INSTRUCTIONS

1. Preheat the oven to 220°C / 428°F.
2. Peel and thoroughly wash the sweet potatoes, then slice them into approximately 5 mm thick rounds.
3. Wash the zucchini and slice lengthwise into approximately 1 cm thick rounds.
4. Drizzle the sliced sweet potatoes and zucchini generously with olive oil and arrange them on the parchment-lined baking tray.
5. Wash and slice the ginger into thicker rounds. Place these ginger slices among the sweet potato slices on the baking tray for added flavor.
6. Bake the vegetables in the oven for about 20-25 minutes or until they turn golden brown.
7. Quark Dip: Wash and chop the parsley. In the small bowl, mix the quark with the chopped parsley. Season with salt, stir well, and keep covered in the refrigerator until ready to serve.
8. Serve everything on a plate.

CHICKEN BREAST WITH PASTA, ROMANESCO, AND CREAM SAUCE

Breakfast **Lunch** Dessert **Dinner**

For 1 person
Preparation time: 30 minutes

INGREDIENTS

- ½ onion
- ¼ bunch parsley
- About 200 g romanesco
- 1 liter water
- Some salt (iodine-free)
- 80 g low-histamine and gluten-free pasta (see notes on page 148)
- Some olive oil (for chicken breast)
- 1 fresh chicken breast
- 1 tbsp olive oil (for cream sauce)
- 100 ml low-histamine and gluten-free vegetable broth
- 50 ml cream
- 1 tbsp cornstarch
- 2 tbsp cold water

INSTRUCTIONS

1. Peel and finely dice the onion. Wash the parsley, shake dry, and finely chop. Wash the romanesco and cut into small florets.
2. Pasta: Bring water to a boil in a pot with some salt. Cook the pasta al dente according to package instructions.
3. Chicken Breast: Heat oil in the frying pan. On high heat, brown the chicken breast on both sides. Reduce heat to medium and continue cooking the chicken breast for another 8-10 minutes. Season with salt to taste.
4. Romanesco: Bring water to a boil, add salt, and cook romanesco florets for about 8 minutes.
5. Cream Sauce: Sauté onions in hot oil until translucent. Add parsley and sauté briefly. Deglaze with vegetable broth and let it simmer briefly. Add cream and let it simmer for 3 minutes.
6. Mix cornstarch with cold water, add to the sauce, until thickens. Season with salt to taste.
7. Serve and enjoy!

CORN COUSCOUS VEGETABLE PAN

Breakfast   **Lunch**   Dessert   **Dinner**

For 1 person
Preparation time: 45 minutes

INGREDIENTS

- 40 g corn couscous (see notes on page 148)
- 150 ml hot (not boiling) water
- 1 tbsp olive oil
- ½ medium zucchini
- 100 g cranberries
- 90 g feta cheese
- ½ onion
- Some olive oil for frying
- Some salt (iodine-free)

INSTRUCTIONS

1. Place couscous in a bowl and pour hot water over it. Add olive oil, stir well, cover, and leave it for about 10 minutes to absorb.
2. Wash the zucchini and cut into small cubes. Dice the feta cheese and finely chop the onion.
3. Heat oil in the frying pan and sauté the onions until golden brown.
4. Add zucchini cubes and sauté for about 5 minutes until lightly browned.
5. Add feta cheese and cranberries to the frying pan, briefly sauté until the feta begins to melt.
6. Transfer the pan mixture to the soaked couscous in the bowl and mix well.
7. Season with salt to taste.
8. Serve and enjoy your corn couscous vegetable pan!

BAKED APPLE WITH CRISPY FILLING

Breakfast   Lunch   **Dessert**   Dinner

For 1 person
Preparation time: 40 minutes

INGREDIENTS

- 2 apples
- Some butter for greasing the baking dish
- 25 g gluten-free oats
- 20 g low-histamine and gluten-free flour (see notes on page 148)
- 2 tbsp coconut sugar
- 2 tbsp maple syrup
- 1 tbsp melted coconut oil

INSTRUCTIONS

1. Preheat the oven to 180°C / 356°F. Grease the baking dish with butter.
2. Wash the apples, remove the cores and stems using an apple corer.
3. Place the prepared apples in the greased ovenproof baking dish.
4. Crispy Filling: In a small bowl, mix oats, flour, and coconut sugar thoroughly. In a seperate bowl, combine maple syrup and melted coconut oil until homogeneous. Then mix the wet ingredients into the dry ingredients.
5. Fill the apple cavities generously with the filling, and distribute any remaining filling around the apples.
6. Bake the filled apples for about 30 minutes until they are tender and the filling is crispy.
7. Remove from the oven and serve.

Tip: My daughter loves these baked apples with a chocolate filling (high in histamine). To treat both of us, I double the amount of apples, fill half with chocolate, and bake them separately in a baking dish.

GLUTEN-FREE CHEESECAKE WITHOUT CRUST

Breakfast   Lunch   **Dessert**   Dinner

For 1 person
Preparation time: 70 minutes

INGREDIENTS

- Some butter
- A little cornstarch
- 150 g frozen sour cherries
- 2 eggs
- 50 g soft butter
- 100 g sugar
- 1 tbsp cornstarch
- 1 tsp vanilla extract
- 1 pack vanilla sugar
- 125 ml cream
- 100 g mascarpone
- 500 g low-fat quark (curd cheese)
- Optional: lemongrass (see notes on page 148)

INSTRUCTIONS

1. Preheat the oven to 180°C / 356°F.
2. Grease the springform pan with butter and sprinkle with cornstarch.
3. Heat the frozen sour cherries in a pot.
4. Separate the eggs. Beat the egg whites in a bowl until stiff peaks form.
5. In a seperate bowl, mix egg yolks with soft butter, sugar, cornstarch, vanilla extract, vanilla sugar, cream, and mascarpone until creamy.
6. Add quark to the mixture. Gently fold in the stiff egg whites and pour into the prepared springform pan.
7. Gently fold the heated sour cherries into the quark mixture.
8. Bake the cake in the oven for 15 minutes at 180°C / 356°F, then reduce the temperature to 150°C / 302°F and bake for another 40 minutes until done.
9. Allow the cake to cool in the springform pan for 2 hours. Run a knife around the edge to loosen it, then transfer to a plate to serve.

- **Recipes with Rice:** If you don't have a rice cooker, you can alternatively prepare rice in a pot. Please pay attention to the exact amount and follow the instructions according to the package insert. For my sticky rice, I visit the Asian shop to buy "Thai Glutinous Rice" from Spoon & Spoon.

- **Cucumber Cottage Cheese Crispbread Recipe:** My favorite low-histamine and gluten-free crispbread is "Wasa Classic Crispbread". I recommend testing the crispbread individually to ensure it is suitable for histamine tolerance.

- **Recipes with Pasta:** When using low-histamine and gluten-free pasta, make sure it is not made from lentils, chickpeas, buckwheat, or similar histamine-rich foods.

- **Asian Chicken Pan with Rice Recipe:** Due to histamine intolerance, packaged and long-stored chicken meat is not ideal. Therefore, I buy it fresh directly from the farm and freeze it in convenient portions. In such cases, thaw the chicken meat in lukewarm water for about 30 minutes before cooking.

- **Recipes with Flour:** For gluten-free and low-histamine flour, it is advisable to ensure that there are no additives (histamine liberators) such as guar gum, carob bean gum, or buckwheat flour. For my low-histamine and gluten-free flour, I use the Organic Universal Flour Mix from Bauckhof. Although it contains guar gum, which is a histamine liberator, the amount relative to the total is small. You should experiment to find the low-histamine and gluten-free flour that suits you best.

- **Pasta with Pesto Recipe:** I deliberately omitted garlic from the pesto because garlic is a histamine liberator. If you tolerate small amounts of garlic, you can puree it together with basil, macadamia nuts, oil, and herbal salt.

- **Corn-Couscous Vegetable Pan Recipe:** Couscous is usually made from wheat and therefore contains gluten. That's why I use corn couscous and sometimes a corn-rice couscous.

- **Gluten-Free Cheesecake without Crust Recipe:** Normally, lemon is added to a cheese cake, which is not possible with histamine intolerance. For those who still want to enjoy the "lemony taste," finely chopped lemongrass is a suitable alternative. Add the lemongrass very finely chopped to the quark mixture.

AFTERWORD

Dear Reader,

With these lines, I bid you farewell and express my sincere gratitude. My journey has been filled with enlightening discoveries, and I deeply hope that my guide has provided you with valuable insights to pave your own path towards a life free from panic attacks.

The knowledge you have gained from this book marks just the beginning of your journey. The path we have walked leads inevitably into the future. You can follow my further experiences, powerful insights, progress, and recipes on my website www.higlutrigger.ch, or on social media platforms like TikTok, Instagram and Facebook.

HiGluTrigger signifies the connection between histamine intolerance and gluten sensitivity as triggers for panic attacks. This book aims not only to impart knowledge but also to illuminate new avenues. My goal was to spare others the suffering I endured by sharing my personal journey openly, offering shortcuts and landmarks to guide others on their own paths.

We must raise awareness and help people recognize how crucial diet and specific intolerances can be in overcoming panic attacks. Doctors should incorporate these insights into their diagnoses to provide the support sufferers need, enabling them to lead fulfilling lives free from the fear of panic attacks.

While you have followed my journey, I wonder: what does your path look like? Let us share our experiences, for together we are strong, capable of learning from each other and offering valuable advice. Your comments and stories are invaluable, as together we form a powerful community. If you know someone struggling with panic attacks, show empathy and be there for them.

Even the smallest support can make a difference. My journey is meant to inspire you, but now it is time for you to discover your own, personal path.

Finally, I wish you much success on your journey to a life free from panic attacks. May your journey be filled with health, hope, and a strong community that always stands by your side.

With gratitude and best wishes for your future,
Yours, Sara

Website: www.higlutrigger.ch
Instagram: higlutrigger
Facebook: HiGluTrigger
TikTok: Higlutrigger

ACKNOWLEDGEMENTS

I would like to extend my heartfelt thanks to my wonderful husband and our beloved daughter, my parents and my dear sister, as well as Nadja and Debora and all my dear friends, for their tireless support and companionship over the years. Special thanks are due to Isabel, Freshta, Franziska, Teresina, and Zeta for their invaluable help in creating this guide.

I also wish to sincerely thank my long-time specialist, Dr. Heiner Gabele, and my naturopath, Johannes Hermiz. Their professional expertise and support in recent years have significantly contributed to my well-being.

Great thanks also go to my biotherapist; without his valuable support and compassionate guidance, my recovery would not have been as successful.

Without the trust and support of these special people, this guide would not have been possible. Thank you from the bottom of my heart!

Sara Müller looks back on an impressive and versatile career. After successfully completing her studies in architecture, she initially worked as an architect before transitioning to the field of business risk management, where she became a recognized speaker. Eventually, she founded her own company, Jobsharing-Consulting MS AG, and published a highly regarded guide on modern work models. At the same time, she became involved in the art scene, exhibiting her works both nationally and internationally.

In addition to her professional and artistic achievements, she initiated the project mammaconnect© to help mothers navigate their daily lives and reduce feelings of loneliness. Her experiences as a mother and entrepreneur also informed guides like the "Guide to Baby-Friendly Cafés."

Despite her numerous successes, Sara Müller faced an intense struggle with panic attacks and anxiety for over 15 years. In her new book, she shares her personal story and illustrates how the right nutrition can significantly impact mental health. She aims to encourage others who are affected and to provide a holistic approach to overcoming panic attacks.

Today, Sara Müller lives with her family in Zurich and actively promotes discussions about mental health and nutrition, particularly in relation to histamine intolerance and gluten sensitivity. She gives lectures and engages on social media to support those in need.

DISCLAIMER

This book does not provide medical, legal, or financial advice. For individual concerns or issues, please consult a qualified professional. The use of the information in this book is at the reader's own risk. The author and publisher are not liable for any potential damages.

The techniques or advice described in this book do not guarantee specific results. Outcomes may vary.

All trademarks and names mentioned in this book are the property of their respective owners. Their inclusion is for informational purposes only and does not imply endorsement or recommendation by the author or publisher. This book contains no legally binding statements. No claims can be made based on the content presented in the book.

The liability of the author and publisher is limited to the purchase price of this book.

Health and Safety Disclaimer

Some of the recipes or techniques in this book may involve handling sharp objects, hot surfaces, or potentially allergenic ingredients. Readers should take proper precautions to avoid injury or harm. The author and publisher are not responsible for any injuries, health problems, or adverse reactions that may occur as a result of following the recipes or using ingredients mentioned in this book. Always follow food safety guidelines and consult a doctor if you have any concerns about specific dietary needs or restrictions.

Accuracy Disclaimer

Every effort has been made to ensure the accuracy of the information in this book. However, the author and publisher cannot guarantee that all facts and events described are completely accurate, as some details may be based on memory, interpretation, or publicly available sources. The author and publisher are not liable for any errors or omissions in the content.

Subjectivity of Advice

The advice, opinions, and viewpoints expressed in this book reflect the personal experiences and insights of the author and are intended for general information purposes only. They may not be suitable for every reader, and results or outcomes may vary based on individual circumstances. Readers are encouraged to use their own judgment and seek professional advice where appropriate.

Copyright and Intellectual Property Disclaimer

All content in this book, including but not limited to text, images, and recipes, is the intellectual property of the author and publisher unless otherwise credited. Unauthorized reproduction, distribution, or use of this content is prohibited without prior written permission from the author or publisher.

Disclaimer on Historical/Cultural Representation

The biographical accounts and cultural references in this book are presented based on the author's understanding and interpretation. They are not intended to provide an exhaustive or definitive history and may reflect the author's perspective. Any perceived inaccuracies are unintended, and readers are encouraged to explore additional sources for broader context.

No Warranty of Results

The strategies, techniques, and suggestions presented in this book are provided without any express or implied warranty of results. The author and publisher make no guarantee of success in any endeavor or activity described in this book, and the reader assumes all responsibility for applying the information presented.

REFERENCES

AAAAI. (November 5, 2022). *American Academy of Allergy, Asthma & Immunology*. https://www.aaaai.org/tools-for-the-public/conditions-library/allergies/celiac-disease

aha! (May 5, 2023). *aha! Allergiezentrum Schweiz*. Fruktosemalabsorption: https://www.aha.ch/allergiezentrum-schweiz/allergien-intoleranzen/nahrungsmittelintoleranzen/fruktosemalabsorption

aha! (May 5, 2023). *aha! Allergiezentrum Schweiz*. Laktoseintoleranz: https://www.aha.ch/allergiezentrum-schweiz/allergien-intoleranzen/nahrungsmittelintoleranzen/laktoseintoleranz

aha!, A. (May 5, 2023). *aha! Allergiezentrum Schweiz*. https://www.aha.ch/allergiezentrum-schweiz/allergien-intoleranzen/nahrungsmittelintoleranzen/zoeliakie-glutenintoleranz

American Academy of Allergy, Asthma & Immunology. (June 12, 2023). https://www.aaaai.org/tools-for-the-public/conditions-library/allergies/celiac-disease

BAG: Michael Beer, J. L. (September 2012). *6. Schweizerischer Ernährungsbericht*. Bundesamt für Gesundheit BAG: https://www.blv.admin.ch/blv/de/home/lebensmittel-und-ernaehrung/publikationen/statistik-und-berichte-ernaehrung.html

Bandelow, B., Boerner, R. J., Kasper, S., Linden, M., Wittchen, H.-U., & Möller, H.-J. (May 10, 2023). *Deutsches Ärzteblatt*. Generalisierte Angststörung: https://www.aerzteblatt.de/archiv/137451/Generalisierte-Angststoerung

Benotmane, D. B. (June 11, 2023). *Info Medizin*. www.infomedizin.de/krankheiten/zoeliakie-glutenunvertraeglichkeit

Biesiekierski, J. R. (2017). *National Library of Medicine*. What is gluten? *Journal of Gastroenterology and Hepatology*. https://pubmed.ncbi.nlm.nih.gov/28244676/

Briden, L. (June 11, 2023). *Lara Briden*. The Period Revolutionary: https://www.larabriden.com/the-curious-link-between-estrogen-and-histamine-intolerance/

Catassi, P. C. (June 12, 2023). *Dr. Schär Institute*. Fachjournal „Nutrients", Glutox-Studie: https://www.drschaer.com/sites/default/files/DSIF_01-2016_DE_16-07-12_Internet_0.pdf

Dr. Schär Institute, L. E. (June 12, 2023). *Dr. Schär Institute, Fachjournal „Nutrients" veröffentlichte Glutox-Studie*. https://www.drschaer.com/sites/default/files/DSIF___16-07-12_Internet_0.pdf

Elli, L., & Tomba, C. (June 12, 2023). *MDPI*. Evidence for the Presence of Non-Celiac Gluten Sensitivity in Patients with Functional Gastrointestinal Symptoms: Results from a Multicenter Randomized Double-Blind Placebo-Controlled Gluten Challenge: https://www.mdpi.com/2072-6643/8/2/84

Elli, L., & Tomba, C. (June 12, 2023). *MDPI, Evidence for the Presence of Non-Celiac Gluten Sensitivity in Patients with Functional Gastrointestinal Symptoms: Results from a Multicenter Randomized Double-Blind Placebo-Controlled Gluten Challenge*. https://www.mdpi.com/2072-6643/8/2/84

Enck, P., & Frieling, T. (2019). *Darm an Hirn! Der geheime Dialog unserer beiden Nervensysteme und sein Einfluss auf unser Leben*. Verlag Herder Spektrum.

Europäische Stiftung für Allergieforschung, ECARF. (April 4, 2023). https://www.ecarf.org/info-portal/allgemeine-allergie-infos/nahrungsmittel-intoleranzen

Ford, D. (May 5, 2023). Das Gluten-Syndrom: Eine neurologische Krankheit! Gluten können das Nervensystem schädigen und neurologische Symptome auslösen. https://www.sciencedirect.com/science/article/abs/pii/S0306987709002230

Halliwill, M. J. (June 13, 2023). *National Library of Medicine*. The Intriguing Role of Histamine in Exercise Responses: https://www.ncbi.nlm.nih.gov/pmc/articles/PMC5161583/

Halliwill, M. J. (June 13, 2023). *National Library of Medicine*. The Intriguing Role of Histamine in Exercise Responses: https://pubmed.ncbi.nlm.nih.gov/27741023/

Heike Alsleben, Rufer, M., & Weiss, A. (2011). *Stärker als die Angst, Ein Ratgeber für Menschen mit Angst- und Panikstörungen und deren Angehörige* (2. Aufl.). Hogrefe AG.

Heilpraktiker, B. D. (June 12, 2023). *Bund Deutscher Heilpraktiker.* https://www.bdh-online.de/welt-zoeliakie-tag-am-16-mai-glutenfrei-trend-erst-testen-dann-verzichten/

Hindernik, E., & Schneider, U. S. (2022). *Welche Farbe hat der Montag? Synästhesie: das Leben mit verknüpften Sinnen.* Hirzel.

Histaminikus. (June 2, 2023). *Histaminikus.* https://histaminikus.de/blogs/histaminfrei-leben/histaminintoleranz

Histaminikus. (June 11, 2023). *Histaminikus.* Hormone und Histaminintoleranz: https://histaminikus.de/blogs/blog/hormone-und-histaminintoleranz

Histaminikus. (April 12, 2023). *Histaminikus.* https://histaminikus.de/blogs/blog/wie-histamin-das-gehirn-beeinflusst

Histaminikus. (October 1, 2023). *Histaminikus.* https://histaminikus.de/blogs/blog/eliminationsdiaet

Histaminintoleranz, H. (June 11, 2023). *Histaminikus.* https://histaminikus.de/blogs/histaminfrei-leben/histaminintoleranz

Histaminta. (June 6, 2023). *Histaminta.* https://histaminta.de

Hochsensibilität, N. (June 2, 2023). *Netzwerk Hochsensibilität.* https://www.netzwerk-hsp.ch/

IQWiG. (December 14, 2022). *Institut für Qualität und Wirtschaftlichkeit im Gesundheitswesen.* Zöliakie (Glutenunverträglichkeit): https://www.gesundheitsinformation.de/gluten-und-weizen-sensitivitaet-allergie-oder-unvertraeglichkeit.html

Koning, F. (June 11, 2023). *PubMed.* Die Nebenwirkungen von Gluten: https://pubmed.ncbi.nlm.nih.gov/26606684/

Mayer, E. (2019). *Das zweite Gehirn.* Riva Verlag ISBN: 9783959713795.

Medizin, I. (June 6, 2023). *Info Medizin.* Lebensmittel mit und ohne Gluten: https://www.infomedizin.de/fileadmin/user_upload/PDF/info-medizin-glutenfreie-lebensmittel.pdf

References

NSW Food Authority. (April 4, 2023). *Allergy and Intolerance*. http://www.foodauthority.nsw.gov.au/foodsafetyandyou/life-events-and-food/allergy-and-intolerance

Schauwecker, M. (May 11, 2023). *Das Potential der Hochsensiblen*. https://www.hochsensibilitaet.ch/

Schemann, M. (January 2020). Wie Nerven unseren Darm steuern: Das Enterische Nervensystem. *Swiss Journal of Nutritional Medicine*.

Schumacher, B. (February 24, 2017). *Ärzte Zeitung*. https://www.aerztezeitung.de/Medizin/Gluten-kann-auch-Reizdarm-verursachen-304819.html

SIGHI. (June 11, 2023). *Swiss Interest Group on Histamine Intolerance*. https://www.histaminintoleranz.ch/de/einleitung_kurzfassung.html

SIGHI. (June 11, 2023). *Swiss Interest Group on Histamine Intolerance, Medikamente*. https://www.histaminintoleranz.ch/de/therapie_medikamente.html

SIGHI. (June 13, 2023). Swiss Interest Group on Histamine Intolerance. Lebensmittellisten für die Histamin-Eliminationsdiät: https://www.histaminintoleranz.ch/downloads/SIGHI-Merkblatt_histaminarmeErnaehrung.pdf

Synästhesie-Gesellschaft, D. (June 2, 2023). *Deutsche Synästhesie-Gesellschaft*. https://www.synaesthesie

Synästhesie-Gesellschaft, D. (June 2, 2023). *Deutsche Synästhesie-Gesellschaft*. https://www.synaesthesie.org/de/synaesthesie

Tribune, M. (March 23, 2017). *Medical Tribune Public*. Laktose-Intoleranz Allergien: https://mt-public.ch/de/nc/home/volltext/news/knochen-und-psyche-in-gefahr/

Universitätsspital, Z. (May 31, 2023). *Universitätsspital Zürich*. https://www.usz.ch/krankheit/angststoerungen/

Wyrsch, D. P. (2020). *Neurosensitivität*.

Zöliakie-Gesellschaft, D. (May 5, 2023). *German Celiac Society e.V.* https://www.dzg-online.de/ Zoller, S. F. (June 2, 2023). *FZ-Consulting*. https://www.fz-consulting.ch/

Zopf, P. (June 11, 2023). *Mein-Allergie-Portal.com.* https://www.mein-allergie-portal.com/zoeliakie-und-glutensensitivitaet/396-zoeliakie-glutensensitivitaet-es-gibt-auch-extraintestinale-symptome.html